USDA

United States
Department of
Agriculture

Forest Service

Pacific Northwest
Research Station

General Technical
Report
PNW-GTR-863

July 2012

Synthesis of Wind Energy Development and Potential Impacts on Wildlife in the Pacific Northwest, Oregon and Washington

Miranda H. Mockrin and Rebecca A. Gravenmier

Authors

Miranda H. Mockrin is a research biologist, Rocky Mountain Research Station, 2150 Centre Avenue, Building A, Fort Collins, CO 80526; and **Rebecca A. Gravenmier** is a natural resource specialist, Pacific Northwest Research Station, 333 SW First Avenue, Portland, OR 97205.

Cover photographs: top left, Dennis E. Schwartz; top right, Paul Cryan, USGS; bottom, Michael Schroeder, WA DFW.

Abstract

Mockrin, Miranda H.; Gravenmier, Rebecca A. 2012. Synthesis of wind
energy development and potential impacts on wildlife in the Pacific Northwest,
Oregon and Washington. Gen. Tech. Rep. PNW-GTR-863. Portland, OR: U.S.
Department of Agriculture, Forest Service, Pacific Northwest Research Station.
55 p.

Nationally, there is growing public interest in and policy pressure for developing
alternative and renewable sources of energy. Wind energy facilities in the Pacific
Northwest expanded rapidly over the past decade, as a result of state policies that
encourage wind energy development. While much of the development thus far
has occurred on private lands, there is interest in expanding onto federal land.
However, there are concerns about the impacts of wind energy on wildlife. Wind
energy facilities have the potential to harm wildlife both directly through collisions with turbines and transmission lines, and indirectly by modifying habitat.
This report synthesizes the available scientific literature on potential wind energy
facility impacts to wildlife, with a focus on the Pacific Northwest (Oregon and
Washington), and summarizes the current best management practices recommended in federal and state guidelines for wind energy development. Research gaps
in our understanding of wind energy impacts on wildlife remain. Future research
needs include long-term, multisite, experimental studies of wind energy impacts
on wildlife, improved ability to estimate population-level and cumulative impacts
of wind energy facilities on wildlife, and better knowledge of key wildlife species'
migration and demography.

Keywords: Wind energy, turbine, wildlife, Pacific Northwest, Oregon,
Washington.

Contents

Introduction

Wind energy development has increased substantially on private land in the Pacific Northwest, and there is growing interest in development on public lands. This report brings together information on wind energy development in the region, potential impacts on wildlife, and best management practices and guidelines for development, to provide federal and state land managers, biologists, and policymakers in the Pacific Northwest with information that can advise policies, land use decisions, or environmental impact analyses. Specifically, we present background information on the structure and operation of wind energy facilities, including associated facilities such as roads and transmission lines. We then summarize current peer-reviewed science pertaining to the effects of wind energy facilities on terrestrial fauna, and provide an overview of current best management practices and recommendations for wind energy development, drawn from federal and state wind energy development guidelines. Best management practices are cross-referenced to peer-reviewed science (where applicable or available). We conclude with a summary of the current research needs for management.

Background on Wind Energy Development

Nationally, there is growing public interest in and policy pressure for developing alternative and renewable sources of energy. In 2010, wind development in the United States increased by over 5,000 megawatts (MW) of new generating capacity, a national rise in capacity of 15 percent to a total of just over 40,000 MW (American Wind Energy Association 2011). This increase fell below growth seen in 2008 and 2009 (increases of more than 8,500 MW and 10,000 MW, respectively), owing in part to changes in federal incentives (American Wind Energy Association 2011). Globally, the United States is one of the fastest growing producers of wind energy, although wind power represents approximately only 2 percent of total U.S. electricity generation (U.S. Department of Energy 2010). Development is expected to continue, and even accelerate, as the U.S.' energy policy emphasizes independence from imported petroleum and reduction of carbon emissions. Wind-generated electrical energy is renewable and has a number of environmental benefits: electricity is produced without air pollution, greenhouse gas emissions, water consumption, mining, waste storage, and other problems associated with many traditional forms of energy generation.

To be effective, wind energy developments must be located in open areas with high windspeeds, with connections to transmission lines. Wind resources are often greatest in uplands, grasslands, and as well as offshore, coastal areas. Nationally, wind resources are greatest in the Midwestern United States from Texas to North

Dakota (U.S. Department of Energy 2008). However, current wind energy facilities are concentrated both in the Midwest and the Western United States, including California, Oregon, and Washington. The decision to site a wind energy facility occurs not just in response to wind resources, but also to electricity pricing, state and local policies, and access to transmission lines (U.S. Department of Energy 2011). In 2010, only seven states had more than 2,000 MW of wind power capacity, including Washington and Oregon (both had just over 2,100 MW online in 2010, ranking them fifth and sixth nationally) (American Wind Energy Association 2011). Wind energy facilities in the Pacific Northwest have grown quickly, partially as a result of favorable state policies that encourage wind energy development, and renewable energy is expected to continue to grow in the region. Oregon law requires utilities to provide 25 percent renewable energy to their customers by 2025, and the state has established goals to reduce greenhouse gas emissions by 75 percent below 1990 levels by 2050 (Oregon Columbia Plateau Ecoregion Wind Energy Taskforce 2008). In 2006, Washington passed legislation requiring 15 percent of the electricity sold in the state by 2020 be derived from renewable sources, with a reduction in greenhouse gas emissions to 50 percent below 1990 levels by 2050 (Washington Department of Fish and Wildlife 2009).

Nationally, development of wind energy facilities has been mostly concentrated on private land. However, there is increasing interest in developing wind energy facilities on federal lands. Under Executive Order 13514, federal agencies are instructed to implement renewable energy projects on federal lands (Executive Order 13514 74 FR 52117, October 8, 2009). Nationally, the U.S. Department of the Interior, Bureau of Land Management (BLM) had 327 MW of installed wind capacity under 25 right-of-way authorizations by January 2009, with another 167 right-of-way authorizations approved (USDI Bureau of Land Mangement 2009). Guidance for BLM's wind energy program was developed through a Westwide planning process that established policies and best management practices for all BLM lands, amending 52 land use plans (USDI Bureau of Land Management 2005). The U.S. Department of Agriculture, Forest Service released final directives for wind energy projects in August 2011 (76 CFR 47354 2011). These internal directives provide standardized direction and guidance for wind energy projects on National Forest System lands (USDA Forest Service 2011a, 2011b). The Forest Service chose not to pursue a national environmental impact assessment and planning process, concluding it would be more efficient to examine individual sites as projects are proposed (76 CFR 47354 2011). The Forest Service currently has no approved wind energy projects, but as of June 2011, had one accepted application for a wind energy project in Vermont, a number of proposals indicating interest in southern California, and 15 meteorological tower/wind energy testing sites nationwide.[1]

In the Pacific Northwest, the majority of wind energy development thus far has also taken place on private lands, much of it concentrated (fig. 1). However, interest in public lands in the region is growing: applications for wind-testing meteorological towers on BLM lands in Oregon and Washington increased from 6 permits per year in 2006 to 24 in 2008 (Morris 2009). By March 2011, BLM lands had one wind energy facility application (0.42 km^2) and 19 meteorological towers, as well as five pending wind energy facility applications (122 km^2), and 16 proposed meteorological towers.[2] The Forest Service has also received proposals for meteorological towers on the Fremont-Winema and Olympic National Forests.[3] One full-scale wind energy facility prospectus has been received by the Forest Service for a 400-MW project in the Fremont-Winema National Forest (up to 175 wind turbines over 260 km^2) (see footnote 3).

Wind energy is likely to continue to grow nationally and regionally on all types of land ownership, which raises concerns about the impacts of wind energy developments on wildlife (Arnett et al. 2008, Kunz et al. 2007b, National Research Council 2007). Wind energy facilities have the potential to harm wildlife both directly through collisions with wind turbines and infrastructure, and indirectly by modifying habitat. Land managers of Pacific Northwest forests and rangelands require information on the effects of wind energy facilities on wildlife and information on the current best management practices, as supported by scientific studies. This report is a synthesis of these potential impacts to wildlife, with a focus on the Pacific Northwest (Oregon and Washington states). After presenting background information on the operation of a wind energy facility and a summary of current peer-reviewed science on the effects of wind energy facilities on the terresterial fauna we present an overview of the guidelines and best practices from the U.S. Fish and Wildlife Service (USFWS), BLM, and Forest Service, and the states of Oregon and Washington, cross-referenced to peer-reviewed science (table 1).

Wind energy is likely to continue to grow nationally and regionally on all types of land ownership, which raises concerns about the impacts of wind energy developments on wildlife.

---

[1] Parker, G. 2011. Personal communication. Realty specialist, Energy Uses, Lands and Realty Management Staff, USDA Forest Service, 1400 Independence Ave., SW, Mailstop 1124, Washington, DC 20250.

[2] Jensen, C. 2011. Personal communication. Lands section chief, Bureau of Land Management, Oregon State Office, 333 SW 1st Avenue, Portland, OR 97204.

[3] Sauser, J. 2011. Personal communication. Regional land use program manager, Lands and Recreation Residence Special Uses, USDA Forest Service, Pacific Northwest Regional Office, 333 SW 1st Avenue, Portland, OR 97204.

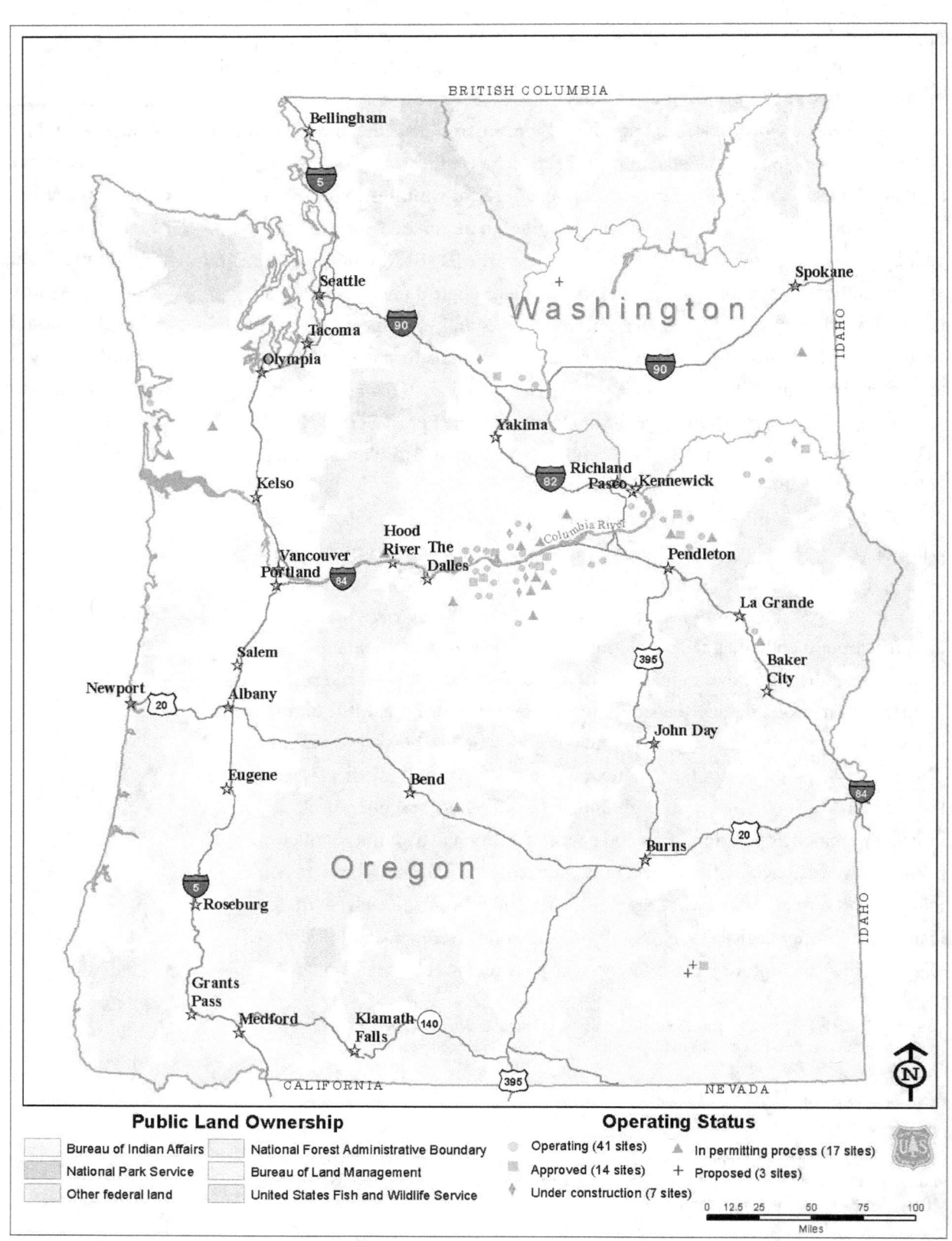

Figure 1—Wind energy projects and status on private land in Oregon and Washington. Data courtesy of Renewable Northwest Project (2011).

Table 1—Best management practices (BMPs), from U.S. Department of the Interior, U.S. Fish and Wildlife Service (USFWS) (2011d), U.S. Department of Agriculture, Forest Service (FS) (2011a,b), U.S. Department of the Interior, Bureau of Land Management (BLM) (2005a,b), Oregon (OR) (Oregon Columbia Plateau Ecoregion Wind Energy Taskforce 2008), and Washington (WA) (Washington Department of Fish and Wildlife 2009)[a]

BMPs to reduce habitat loss and avoidance	Source	concern	Resource Citation/reference
Establish nondisturbance buffer zones to protect sensitive habitats or areas of high risk for species of concern identified in preconstruction studies. Determine the extent of the buffer zone in consultation with the USFWS and state, local, and tribal wildlife biologists, and land management agencies (e.g., BLM and FS) or other credible experts as appropriate.	USFWS	Sensitive habitats, species of concern	Buffer zones would differ with species. References for sage grouse literature include Connelly et al. 2000, Naugle et al. 2011 and Walker et al. 2007.
Restore wildlife habitat temporarily disturbed during the construction, maintenance, or repair of the project. Minimize habitat disturbance before and during construction. From USFWS: "Use available data from state and federal agencies, and other sources (which could include maps or databases), that show the location of sensitive resources and the results of Tier 2 and/or Tier 3 studies to establish the layout of roads, power lines, fences, and other infrastructure."	USFWS, FS, BLM, and OR	Wildlife habitat	Standard operating procedure.
Mitigate temporary and permanent impacts to wildlife habitat and populations. See appropriate guidelines for more specific information on mitigation. Private developers and federal managers will have to work with the USFWS to comply with relevant legislation for some species (Endangered Species Act, Bald and Golden Eagle Protection Act, Migratory Bird Treaty Act).	USFWS, FS, BLM, OR, and WA	Wildlife habitat	Standard operating procedure.
Avoid or minimize construction during periods when it will disturb wildlife (e.g., avian nesting season or winter for overwintering game).	FS, BLM, and OR	Wildlife, generally	Standard operating procedure.
Reduce fire hazards. Exact guidance differs among guidelines. For USFWS, "Reduce fire hazard from vehicles and human activities… Site development and operation plans should specifically address the risk of wildfire and provide appropriate cautions and measures to be taken in the event of a wildfire."	USFWS, FS, OR, and WA	Wildlife habitat	Standard operating procedure.

Table 1—Best management practices (BMPs), from U.S. Department of the Interior, U.S. Fish and Wildlife Service (USFWS) (2011d), U.S. Department of Agriculture, Forest Service (FS) (2011a,b), U.S. Department of the Interior, Bureau of Land Management (BLM) (2005a,b), Oregon (OR) (Oregon Columbia Plateau Ecoregion Wind Energy Taskforce 2008), and Washington (WA) (Washington Department of Fish and Wildlife 2009)[a] (continued)

BMPs to reduce habitat loss and avoidance	Source	Resource concern	Citation/reference
Instruct personnel to avoid harassment or disturbance of wildlife.	USFWS, FS, BLM, OR, and WA	Wildlife	Standard operating procedure.
Reduce the introduction and spread of invasive plants, using applicable local policies (e.g., use native species when seeding or planting during restoration, cleaning vehicles and equipment arriving from areas with known invasive species issues, using locally sourced topsoil, and monitoring for and rapidly removing noxious weeds at least annually). Utilize pest and weed control measures as specified by county or state requirements, or by applicable federal agency requirements (such as Integrated Pest Management) when federal policies apply.	USFWS, FS, BLM OR, WA	Wildlife habitat	Standard operating procedure.
Minimize, to the extent practicable, building new roads and infrastructure. Use existing roads and infrastructure when feasible.	USFWS, FS, BLM, and OR	Wildlife	Standard operating procedure.
Use explosives at specified distances to sensitive wildlife or streams and lakes, as established by appropriate agency.	BLM	Wildlife, aquatic resources	Standard operating procedure.
Minimize stream crossings (OR) and avoid impact to hydrology and stream morphology, especially where federal- or state-listed aquatic or riparian species may be involved (USFWS). All guidelines mention the Clean Water Act and water quality. More specific text within OR and USFWS. From USFWS, "Minimize impacts to wetlands and water resources by following all applicable provisions of the Clean Water Act (33 USC 1251-1387) and the Rivers and Harbors Act (33 USC 301 et 16 seq.); for instance, by developing and implementing a storm water management plan and taking measures to reduce erosion and avoid delivery of road-generated sediment into streams and waters."	USFWS, FS, OR, and WA	Aquatic resources	Standard operating procedure.
Follow federal and state measures for handling toxic substances to minimize danger to water and wildlife resources from spills.	USFWS	Wildlife, aquatic resources	Standard operating procedure.
Manage vehicles and traffic volumes to reduce wildlife disturbance.	USFWS, BLM, OR, and WA	Wildlife	Standard operating procedure.

Table 1—Best management practices (BMPs), from U.S. Department of the Interior, U.S. Fish and Wildlife Service (USFWS) (2011d), U.S. Department of Agriculture, Forest Service (FS) (2011a,b), U.S. Department of the Interior, Bureau of Land Management (BLM) (2005a,b), Oregon (OR) (Oregon Columbia Plateau Ecoregion Wind Energy Taskforce 2008), and Washington (WA) (Washington Department of Fish and Wildlife 2009)[a] (continued)

BMPs to reduce direct mortality	Source	Resource concern	Citation/reference
Minimize construction and management practices that may attract wildlife, both prey and predators, to the wind energy facility. Manage garbage, animal carcasses, and structure construction and management practices to avoid increasing wildlife density and raptor activity at the wind energy facility (e.g., avoid increasing prey populations through vegetation manipulation, as that may increase raptors) (BLM), avoid habitat enhancements such as nesting platform or nest boxes, ponds, guzzlers, etc. (USFWS).	USFWS, BLM, and WA	Wildlife, raptors	Standard operating procedure. Raptor information from Smallwood et al. 2009, Smallwood and Thelander 2008.
Locate turbines to avoid separating bird and bat species of concern from their daily roosting, feeding, or nesting sites, if documented that the turbines' presence poses a risk to species (USFWS).	USFWS and BLM	Birds and bats	Standard operating procedure. Research thus far shows that turbines primarily strike migratory bats (not local roosting colonies) (Arnett et al. 2008).
All guidelines state that bird perching should be discouraged. From OR, "Anti-perching devices should be installed on transmission pole tops and cross arms where the poles are located within 0.5 mile of turbines."	USFWS, FS, BLM, OR, and WA	Birds, specifically, raptors	Problems with bird perching reviewed in Avian Power Line Interaction Committee (2006).
Avoid use of guy wires on permanent meteorological towers. From USFWS guidelines: "If guy wires are necessary, bird flight diverters or high visibility marking devices should be used."	USFWS, FS, BLM, OR, and WA	Birds	Longcore et al. 2008.
All guidelines discuss BMPs for reducing avian collisions from power lines. From USFWS, "Place low and medium voltage connecting power lines associated with the wind energy development underground to the extent possible, unless burial of the lines is prohibitively expensive (e.g., where shallow bedrock exists) or where greater adverse impacts to biological resources would result." USFWS guidelines provide more information on when overhead lines may be acceptable and recommend that to the extent possible Avian Power Line Interaction Committee 2006 guidelines be followed for overhead lines, aboveground low and medium voltage lines, transformers, and conductors.	USFWS, FS, BLM, OR, and WA	Birds	Avian Power Line Interaction Committee 2006, Longcore et al. 2008.

Table 1—Best management practices (BMPs), from U.S. Department of the Interior, U.S. Fish and Wildlife Service (USFWS) (2011d), U.S. Department of Agriculture, Forest Service (FS) (2011a,b), U.S. Department of the Interior, Bureau of Land Management (BLM) (2005a,b), Oregon (OR) (Oregon Columbia Plateau Ecoregion Wind Energy Taskforce 2008), and Washington (WA) (Washington Department of Fish and Wildlife 2009)[a] (continued)

BMPs to reduce direct mortality	Source	concern	Resource Citation/reference
Regulations on lighting are addressed in multiple guidelines. If a structure is over 200 m, lighting will be required by the Federal Aviation Administration (FAA), but there are specific suggestions for type of lighting to use within USFWS and OR guidelines. From USFWS, "Employ only red, or dual red and white strobe, strobe-like, or flashing lights, not steady burning lights, to meet FAA requirements for visibility lighting of wind turbines, permanent meteorological towers, and communication towers. Only a portion of the turbines within the wind project should be lighted, and all pilot warning lights should fire synchronously." Detailed direction in FS directives as well. Note: BLM guidelines also recommend minimizing lighting to reduce visual disturbance. Wildlife impacts are not specifically mentioned.	USFWS, FS, BLM, and OR.	Birds	Information on lighting and birds: Gehring et al. 2009, Kerlinger et al. 2010, Longcore et al. 2008. Horn et al. (2008) found no impact for bats between lighted and unlighted turbines (lit with steady and strobing aviation obstruction lights).
Keep lighting at both operation and maintenance facilities and substations to the minimum required. From USFWS: a. Use lights with motion or heat sensors and switches to keep lights off when not required. b. Lights should be hooded downward and directed to minimize horizontal and skyward illumination. c. Minimize use of high-intensity lighting, steady-burning, or bright lights such as sodium vapor, quartz, halogen, or other bright spotlights. d. All internal turbine nacelle and tower lighting should be extinguished when unoccupied. USFWS guidelines specify that guidance is for buildings within half a mile of turbine.	USFWS, BLM, FS, and OR	Birds	For birds (Gehring et al. 2009, Kerlinger et al. 2010 Longcore et al. 2008) Kerlinger et al. (2010) found no difference in bird mortalities between turbines lit with flashing lights and unlit turbines. Horn et al. (2008) found no impact for bats between lighted and unlighted turbines (lit with steady and strobing aviation obstruction lights).
Manage vehicles and traffic volumes to reduce wildlife collisions	USFWS, BLM, OR, and WA	Wildlife	Standard operating procedure.

[a] Practices are organized by resource, and listed with supporting scientific literature, where applicable.

Description of a Wind Energy Facility

Utility-scale wind turbines (those that can generate greater than 1 MW) installed after the 1990s have all been similarly designed with a single tubular tower ranging in height from 60 to 100 m, and three rotor blades up to 40 to 50 m in length (Kunz et al. 2007b, U.S. Department of Energy 2008) (fig. 2, 3). Current turbine rotor blades may reach up to 50 m (power outputs of 3 to 5 MW) (U.S. Department of Energy 2008), so that tower plus blade height ranges up to 150 m, taller than a 40-story building (Kunz et al. 2007b). Over the past 25 years, wind turbine size has steadily increased, in part because windspeed increases with the height above the ground, enabling larger turbines to produce energy more efficiently.

Turbines work by converting energy from the moving rotor blades into electrical power in the nacelle, a unit at the top of the tower that houses the converter and controls. Sensors on the turbine provide information on windspeed and component performance in order to respond to windspeed and regulate the power output and rotor speed. The turbine is pointed into the wind by rotating the nacelle around the tower. Turbine power output is controlled by changing the "pitch" or angle of the blades around their long axis in response to wind. Turbines generally start producing power in winds of 3.5 to 4.0 m per second (m/s) (Arnett et al. 2011, Baerwald et al. 2009), reaching maximum power output at about 12.5 to 13.4 m/s (U.S. Department of Energy 2008). The amount of energy available for turbines increases with the cube (the third power) of windspeed, meaning that a 10 percent increase in windspeed creates a larger (33 percent) increase in available energy. When windspeed becomes too high, at approximately 23 m/s, turbines will "pitch" or "feather" the blades to stop rotation and halt power production. Each 1.5-MW turbine may produce 4.6 million kilowatt-hours per year, equivalent to electricity needs for 300 to 900 households, depending on energy consumption (National Wind Coordinating Collaborative 2010). A turbine's MW rating is the "name-plate" capacity or manufacturer's capacity of a wind turbine to generate electricity. The actual energy produced by a turbine will depend on the windspeeds experienced at the site.

Within a wind energy facility, individual turbines are normally arranged in a line linked together through underground cables into arrays, then connected to the local power grid. Turbines are typically installed in arrays of 30 to 150 (U.S. Department of Energy 2008). Although the footprint, or area occupied by a turbine, is generally small (usually 2800 to 4050 m^2 per turbine),[4] turbines are only part of the infrastructure developed for a wind energy facility. The associated buildings,

> Over the past 25 years, wind turbine size has steadily increased, in part because windspeed increases with the height above the ground, enabling larger turbines to produce energy more efficiently.

---

[4] Strickland, D. 2011. Personal communication. President and senior ecologist, Western EcoSystems Technology, Inc., Environmental and Statistical Consultants, 2003 Central Avenue, Cheyenne, WY 82001.

Dennis E Schwartz

Paul Cryan, U.S. Geological Survey

Figure 2—Operational wind turbines.

Figure 3—Construction and maintenance of wind turbines.

roads, electrical transmission lines, or connections to electrical transmission lines make up the wider footprint of a wind energy facility. Access roads may be the largest infrastructure development for a wind energy facility because each turbine requires an access road so that turbines can be serviced. Access roads are used by heavy equipment, including cement mixers and cranes, for construction and maintenance. Depending upon the project, roads will be a minimum of 3 m wide, and may extend up to 10 m. In total, the permanent footprint of a wind energy facility is approximately 5 to 10 percent of the entire site (USDI Bureau of Land Management 2005). The amount of surface disturbance will differ with site characteristics such as vegetation and topography. The current trend has been to locate wind energy facilities where there are existing transmission lines that can be used. In the future, if wind power is to increase significantly, there will need to be substantial expansion of transmission systems to deliver wind energy through the electrical grid (U.S. Department of Energy 2011, USDI Bureau of Land Management 2005).

> **Construction of a wind energy facility causes habitat loss and fragmentation when vegetation is removed for infrastructure development, including turbines, buildings, roads, and connections from the wind energy facility to the existing electrical transmission lines.**

Science Findings: The Effects of Wind Energy Facilities on Wildlife

The first wind energy facilities were constructed in the United States in the 1980s in California, and concerns about wildlife collisions emerged soon thereafter. The wind industry has grown tremendously over the past 10 years, leading to additional concerns about habitat alteration. Because it is a new form of land use, there has been relatively little research on the impacts of wind energy facilities on wildlife, but new studies are continuously emerging. Below, we review the current scientific literature on wind energy facilities and wildlife, considering habitat loss and direct mortality, in sequence.

Habitat Loss and Modification

Construction of a wind energy facility causes habitat loss and fragmentation when vegetation is removed for infrastructure development, including turbines, buildings, roads, and connections from the wind energy facility to the existing electrical transmission lines. Operation of wind turbines and associated human activity may also reduce wildlife habitat quality, either negatively affecting resident wildlife populations or displacing populations (Arnett et al. 2008, Kunz et al. 2007b, Kuvlesky et al. 2007, Pearce-Higgins et al. 2012). The overall impact of wind energy facilities on habitat depends upon the habitat quality and wildlife community prior to facility construction (U.S. Fish and Wildlife Service 2012). Although agricultural areas can offer significant benefits for some wildlife species, a wind energy facility built in an agricultural area will cause less destruction of native vegetation than will a facility built in forested vegetation. Similarly, constructing a wind energy facility in natural vegetation with low levels of human use will lead to increased human activity, noise, and lighting, whereas an agricultural area may already have significant human use and infrastructure.

Most of the habitat loss from wind energy facility construction results from the creation of a road network between turbines, which is needed for both construction and maintenance. Roads reduce natural vegetation, while introducing disturbance in the form of noise, lights, pollution, and human activity (roads also increase direct mortality through collisions) (Fahrig and Rytwinski 2009). Prior research shows that aquatic organisms may be affected by road construction owing to changes in geomorphic processes, including sedimentation during construction and use during the life of the road (Gucinski et al. 2001, Switalski et al. 2004, Trombulak and Frissell 2000). Beyond the direct changes associated with wind energy facility construction and operation, wind energy facilities may also lead to greater indirect effects on habitat that play out over longer timeframes, such as introduction of invasive species, alteration of fire regimes, and increased predator populations (U.S. Fish and Wildlife Service 2012).

In an operating wind energy facility, new roads and associated human activity, along with the noise, lighting, and movement of the turbines combine to modify the environment for wildlife. The effects of this habitat modification on wildlife remain unclear for many species, as there have been relatively few studies of wildlife after wind energy facility operation, with still fewer studies conducted over long time-frames. Most studies of wildlife response to wind energy facility operation have been relatively brief, and often focus on specific effects on behavior or abundance, rather than the population-level impacts of disturbance (Carrete et al. 2009, Madsen and Boertmann 2008). There are far more general studies (i.e., not specific to wind energy facilities) of species' avoidance of roads and traffic disturbances (Fahrig and Rytwinski 2009, Gucinski et al. 2001, Trombulak and Frissell 2000). This literature on wildlife and roads shows that roads have consistently negative impacts on a wide range of taxa, through direct mortality, vegetation alterations, and disturbance caused by human activity (noise, lights, traffic motion) (Fahrig and Rytwinski 2009). Species most affected by direct mortality on roads include reptiles and amphibians, as well as some mid-sized and larger mammals with low reproductive rates and large movement ranges (although small mammals generally showed either neutral or positive impacts) (Fahrig and Rytwinski 2009).

Habitat loss resulting from noise is often associated with roads, but wind turbine noise has also been discussed in the literature on wildlife and wind energy. However, while human acceptance of wind turbine noise has been a major area of research (Hessler and Hessler 2011), relatively little research has been done specifi-cally on turbine noise impacts on wildlife. Maximum allowed noise for human exposure is generally around the 40 dB(A)[5] level (Knopper and Ollson 2011), but wildlife are known to be sensitive to noise. Grouse species, in particular, are often discussed in the literature about noise (BLM 2005b, Manville 2004). Barber et al. (2010) stated that -20 dBA is the level of sound just audible to many species (e.g., bats, owls, or foxes). Although species' responses to noise disturbance will differ, bird distribution and physiological responses to sound are documented to occur between 40 to 60 dBA (Barber et al. 2010, Reijnen et al. 1996). Data suggest noise increases of 3 to 10 dBA correspond to 30- to 90-percent reductions in alerting distances for wildlife, respectively (Barber et al. 2010). Only the Forest Service guidelines mention a specific threshold for noise, stating not to exceed 10 dB above the background noise level "in or near habitat of wildlife known to be sensitive to noise during reproduction, roosting, or hibernation; or where habitat abandonment may be an issue;" however, guidelines do not provide specific scientific studies linked to this threshold (USDA Forest Service, 2011a). Understanding the potential effects of turbine noise on wildlife will require additional research (U.S. Fish and Wildlife Service 2012), although it remains challenging to isolate noise effects from associated disturbances (e.g., isolating turbine noise from the visual stimulation of turbine movement).

Because wind energy facility development has expanded rapidly in recent decades, there are still relatively few studies of their effects on wildlife populations in the Pacific Northwest region. In this region, concerns about habitat loss and alteration owing to wind energy facility development are likely to focus on endangered or high-profile species and habitats of conservation significance, including northern spotted owls (*Strix occidentalis caurina*) and marbled murrelets (*Brachyramphus marmoratus*) in old-growth forest, and greater sage grouse (*Centrocercus urophasianus*), pygmy rabbits (*Brachylagus idahoensis*), and ground squirrels (*Urocitellus* spp.) in shrub steppe vegetation. Across the region, land use impacts on bull trout (*Salvelinus confluentus*) and anadromous fishes are also of concern. With the exception of sage grouse, discussed below, the effects of wind energy facilities on these species have not yet been studied. Below we review the current scientific literature on the effects of habitat loss and modification on wildlife, incorporating information from the Pacific Northwest when available.

Birds—

Among bird species, songbirds and grassland birds are the primary species negatively affected by the disturbance of wind energy facilities and roads (Fahrig and

---

[5] A decibel (dB) is a unit of measurement of voltage or other intensity. Decibles are one tenth of a bel.

Rytwinski 2009). With wind energy development, grassland birds have been the focus of much scientific concern because grassland vegetation has been extensively fragmented by other land uses and because grassland birds have experienced significant population declines (greater than other bird groups) (Arnett et al. 2007). At the Buffalo Ridge wind site in Minnesota, lower songbird densities observed in areas with turbines were thought to result from avoidance of turbines, although exact mechanisms are unclear (Leddy et al. 1999, Osborn et al. 1998). While more research is needed, available studies suggest that some disturbance or displacement may occur for grassland/shrub-steppe species (Arnett et al. 2007).

Nationally, impacts of wind energy facilities on grouse species are of concern because a number of these grassland-dependent species are endangered or declining, and research thus far indicates that grouse are sensitive to anthropogenic activity associated with wind energy facilities (Connelly et al. 2000, U.S. Fish and Wildlife Service 2012). Greater sage grouse found in the eastern parts of Oregon and Washington is a candidate species under the Endangered Species Act (ESA) (75 CFR 13910 2010). While impacts of wind energy facilities on sage grouse are a management concern, there have been relatively few studies of wind energy impacts on sage grouse published in the scientific literature (for review of the literature, including unpublished studies, see Johnson and Holloran [2010] and Naugle et al. [2011]). Research on sage grouse suggests that roads, transmission lines, and areas of oil and gas development and production within 4.8 or 8 km (or more) of active sage grouse leks (breeding grounds) may have significant negative impacts for grouse populations, by reducing fecundity (Connelly et al. 2000, Harju et al. 2010, Naugle et al. 2011, Walker et al. 2007) and yearling survival (Holloran et al. 2010). Disturbances that cause males and females to abandon leks include development of power lines and roads, traffic noise, other human activity and noise, and raptors perching on power lines, as reviewed by Naugle et al. (2011). As development continues, impacts on sage grouse appear to intensify: breeding is disrupted with lower densities of energy development, and populations decrease and avoid areas with higher levels of development (Naugle et al. 2011). Changes in sage grouse populations may emerge in complex ways over time as impacts to breeding and yearlings cause lagged population responses to development and development intensifies over time (Harju et al. 2010, Holloran et al. 2010). Lastly, other types of energy development that result in large-scale manipulation or disturbance of surface water, such as coalbed methane extraction, have also been associated with an increase in West Nile virus among sage grouse, as the additional standing water increases mosquito populations (Naugle et al. 2011). Wind energy development uses some water during construction, but does not require standing water during wind

Nationally, impacts of wind energy facilities on grouse species are of concern because a number of these grassland-dependent species are endangered or declining, and research thus far indicates that grouse are sensitive to anthropogenic activity associated with wind energy facilities.

turbine operation, so West Nile virus should be less of a concern in wind energy operations.

Several studies have discussed habitat avoidance after wind energy facility establishment. A wind energy facility in an agricultural area of the Midwest showed a 47 percent decrease in raptor abundance after establishment of a facility (Garvin et al. 2011). In Norway, researchers found that vacant territories near wind turbines led to decreased breeding success for white-tailed eagles (*Haliaeetus albicilla*) (Dahl et al. 2012). Researchers were not able to differentiate vacancies caused by disturbance or mortality, but showed that vacant territories remained over a 10-year study period (i.e., territories were not recolonized), suggesting that wind turbine operation led to habitat loss.

In coastal areas and wetlands, waterbirds, including flocking geese, swans, ducks, and waders are also considered sensitive to wind energy facility development, generally avoiding wind energy facilities by distances of 100 m or more (Madsen and Boertmann 2008, Masden et al. 2009a). Studies of long-term impacts show mixed results: Madsen and Boertmann (2008) found that pink-footed geese (*Anser brachyrhynchus*) in Denmark reduced their avoidance to relatively small-scale wind energy facilities over an 8-year period, while in a meta-analysis of wind energy facilities, Stewart et al. (2007) found that decreases in bird abundance remained over time. There are concerns that migratory birds face increasing energetic consequences of avoiding wind energy facilities as facilities expand along migratory routes. The energetic costs of avoiding one wind energy facility are small in comparison to a long-distance migratory event, but the population impacts of additional energy costs incurred by avoidance remain unknown (Masden et al. 2009b). In the Pacific Northwest, the marbled murrelet is a coastal species listed as endangered under ESA, but there are not yet any operating wind energy projects within marbled murrelet range, so it is unclear how or if marbled murrelets may avoid wind turbines (Cooper and Sanzenbacher 2006, Nations and Erickson 2009, Nelson et al. 2009).

Nonvolant mammals—

Regarding mammals, there have only been limited studies examining habitat loss and response to wind energy facilities. One study of elk (*Cervus canadensis*) during construction and operation of a wind energy facility in Oklahoma demonstrated that resident elk showed no significant changes in home range or dietary quality (Walter et al. 2006). Elk freely crossed the gravel roads developed for the facility. However, previous studies of road networks have shown that elk tend to avoid large roads, with avoidance increasing with human activity (Wisdom et al. 2000). Elk are also known to be sensitive to human activity away from roads, such as off-road

There are concerns that migratory birds face increasing energetic consequences of avoiding wind energy facilities as facilities expand along migratory routes. The energetic costs of avoiding one wind energy facility are small in comparison to a long-distance migratory event, but the population impacts of additional energy costs incurred by avoidance remain unknown.

recreation (Naylor et al. 2009). Other forms of energy development, including oil and gas development, have been shown to affect ungulates. In one study, mule deer (*Odocoileus hemionus*) avoided areas with energy development, and did not habituate to these areas over a 3-year period, so that indirect habitat loss caused by human activity was far larger than habitat loss resulting from direct vegetation modification during well-pad development (Sawyer et al. 2006).

Small mammals are generally thought to be more resilient in the face of infrastructure development. One study of California ground squirrels showed that animals were able to live among turbines in a wind energy facility (Rabin et al. 2006). However, researchers suggested that the noise of operating turbines led animals to alter their behavior: in a comparison between a control and a turbine site, animals at the turbine site showed greater vigilance and antipredator behavior, which authors concluded was an attempt to compensate for the difficulty of responding to auditory communication within the wind energy facility site. Similar to many other studies of noise disturbance, this study examined behavior between a wind energy facility site and a control site, and thus was not able to isolate specific features of turbine noise from other visual or auditory disturbances in the wind turbine site.

Bats—

The effects of habitat modification by wind energy development on bats are not well understood, but most concerns center around changes in forest vegetation (National Research Council 2007). Wind energy development in forested areas may influence the availability of tree roosts through vegetation modification. Alternatively, researchers have also suggested that because bats use edge habitat between forest and nonforested areas, wind energy development may lead to higher bat activity at the site, and more collisions.

Direct Mortality and Behavior

In addition to habitat modifications, wind energy facilities may directly affect wildlife populations through collision with turbines. Wind turbine collision issues have been most well-studied in birds, particularly raptors and migratory birds, but over the past decade, bat mortality at wind energy facilities has emerged as a significant conservation issue, so that "what was once a bird issue has become a bat issue" as well (Barclay et al. 2007).

Collision issues are essentially the opposite of displacement: species that can tolerate or are even attracted to wind energy facilities are at risk of increased collision mortality, while species that avoid or are displaced by wind energy facilities lose habitat, but do not risk collisions. For example, territorial bird species, such as raptors, may have fewer issues with displacement by wind energy facilities, but then

Collision issues are essentially the opposite of displacement: species that can tolerate or are even attracted to wind energy facilities are at risk of increased collision mortality, while species that avoid or are displaced by wind energy facilities lose habitat, but do not risk collisions.

suffer higher incidence of collisions (Carrete et al. 2009). Conversely, birds that are sensitive to wind energy sites (e.g., grassland birds), and thus avoid them may be less prone to collisions with turbines (Leddy et al. 1999, Osborn et al. 1998). The relationship between the two potential responses (avoidance or collision) may also differ over time (e.g., birds may habituate to a disturbance, or might grow intolerant over time as tolerant individuals are killed and not replaced) (Madders and Whitfield 2006). In addition, risk of collision from wind turbines is not the only source of direct mortality at wind energy sites. For example, although sage grouse are not considered highly at risk from direct mortality with moving turbines, collisions with power lines and vehicles will increase mortality of birds in leks (Naugle et al. 2011).

While direct mortality from collisions is commonly discussed in the wind energy literature, bird mortality caused by collisions with wind turbines is likely much less than collisions with other infrastructure, such as buildings, high-tension lines, and communication towers. Estimates of the latter collisions are difficult to determine, owing to multiple sources of uncertainty, but are thought to be in the hundreds of millions, while total estimates of birds killed by wind turbines are much lower (National Research Council 2007). There is less background information on bat collision rates with other infrastructure, but Johnson et al. (2003) summarize the literature and report relatively low levels of mortality from collisions with other infrastructure. However, bat fatalities from turbines occur in addition to a number of other threats to bat populations, including white-nose syndrome, a rapidly spreading and highly fatal fungal disease that originated in the Northeastern United States (Frick et al. 2010). Bats are also relatively slow reproducing animals, leading to concerns about the ultimate population-level impact of direct mortality from wind turbines (Kunz et al. 2007b).

Because the likelihood of collisions depends upon complex interactions among site characteristics, turbine characteristics, and animal behavior (Kuvlesky et al. 2007, Madders and Whitfield 2006, Stewart et al. 2007), below we discuss each factor for both birds and bats. We consider only the impacts of wind turbines, and not associated transmission lines. Although transmission lines result in additional mortality for bird species through collisions and electrocution, there are existing guidelines on minimizing power line impacts on wildlife (Avian Power Line Interaction Committee 2006) (referenced in current state and federal guidelines (table 1), and power lines are not unique to wind energy facilities. Similarly, management practices for energy corridors have been broadly addressed by the federal Westwide energy corridor planning process (USDE and USDI 2008).

Birds—

Concerns about bird collisions first emerged at wind facilities built in the 1980s in California, where high densities of resident and migratory raptors and smaller turbines (14 to 43 m) with an older "lattice" tower design contributed to an estimated annual fatalities of 1,127 raptors and 2,710 birds (National Research Council 2007, Smallwood and Thelander 2008). Subsequent studies from other parts of the country with more modern turbines have found lower bird fatalities (Barclay et al. 2007, Kuvlesky et al. 2007). The National Research Council (2007) compiled a number of unpublished studies to examine wildlife collisions, using only data from studies that were longer than a year in duration and used standardized mortality searches, including correcting for carcass decomposition, scavenging, and observer search efficiency. This review found that fatalities at wind farms ranged from 0.95 birds/MW/year to 11.7 birds/MW/year (National Research Council 2007). However, subsequent studies at the site with the high estimate (Buffalo Mountain, Tennessee) lowered bird fatality estimates to 1.1 birds/MW/study period (Young and Poulton 2009). The second highest estimate of bird fatality compiled by the National Research Council (2007) was 5.93 birds/MW/year, from Buffalo Mountain, Minnesota. Research indicates that passerines (songbirds), especially nocturnal migrants, are the most frequent collision fatalities across sites. Raptor research in both the United States and Europe shows that raptor fatalities do not follow directly from raptor abundance, because some species-specific behaviors such as flying in rotor-swept areas result in higher collision rates for less common species (de Lucas et al. 2008, Garvin et al. 2011).

Understanding the population-level effects of these collisions requires information on species abundance and distribution, as well as the combined effects of other wind energy facilities. At the individual facility level, estimates of passerine fatalities, from published and unpublished studies, are often below five animals/turbine/year, a level that is thought to be insignificant for populations unless a species is threatened or in decline (Kuvlesky et al. 2007). Raptor populations, in contrast, are thought to be more severely affected by collision mortality because they are longer lived with lower reproductive potential (Carrete et al. 2009). However, population stability is difficult to assess and may require information on dispersal and links between wildlife populations. For example, a 7-year study of the golden eagle (*Aquila chrysaetos*) population at Altamont Pass Wind Resource Area in California documented 42 fatalities from wind turbine strikes (Hunt 2002). Authors concluded that overall population growth was stable, but likely was not producing a surplus of "floater" animals without territories that could buffer the population from additional losses of habitat or increased mortality. More information on links between

Understanding the population-level effects of these collisions requires information on species abundance and distribution, as well as the combined effects of other wind energy facilities.

this population and other populations in the region would help determine population stability (Smallwood and Thelander 2008).

In the Pacific Northwest, there is little peer-reviewed information on avian-wind energy facility collisions, but a number of efforts have compiled technical reports that followed standard search protocols and methods for estimating mortalities in the Columbia Plateau ecoregion, the roughly triangular shaped, that and agricultural region centered around the Columbia River, reaching from the Dalles, Oregon to Lewiston, Idaho to Okanogan, Washington near the Candian border. Much of the wind energy development in Oregon and Washington is concentrated in this region. These wind energy facilities are all located in grassland or agricultural areas. In the most recent synthesis, raptor mortality was on average 0.08/MW/year in the Columbia Plateau ecoregion, and all bird mortality 2.36/MW/year (Johnson and Erickson 2011). At individual wind energy sites, raptor mortality ranged from 0/MW/year to a maximum of 0.29/MW/year, while overall bird mortality ranged from 0.06/MW/year to 7.72/MW/year (Johnson and Erickson 2011).

Bird fatalities were predominantly passerines (68 percent), with 13 percent upland gamebirds, 9 percent raptors, and the remaining 10 percent composed of doves/pigeons, waterbirds, vultures, and other species. The most frequently killed passerine was the horned lark (*Eremophila alpestris*), making up 30.8 percent of all bird fatalities. Horned larks are the most abundant songbird observed during preconstruction bird-use surveys at these sites. Raptor mortality ranged from 0 to 0.29 birds/MW/year, with kestrels (*Falco* spp.) and red-tailed hawks (*Buteo jamaicensis*) as the most commonly killed species (29 percent and 22 percent of all raptors, respectively). In one well-publicized incident, the first golden eagle fatality from a wind turbine in Washington state was reported in May 2009 (Associated Press 2009). In comparison to other regions of the country, the Pacific Northwest had more coots and rails and gamebirds among fatalities, and fewer passerines (National Research Council 2007). Authors conclude that anticipated cumulative effects of current and proposed wind energy facilities will be low on the common grassland and agricultural species that are the majority of fatalities in the Columbia Plateau ecoregion (Johnson and Erickson 2011). For less common species, authors use survey data from the Breeding Bird Survey and available information on natural mortality rates to also conclude that for the Columbia Plateau ecoregion, more rarely killed species are also unlikely to incur significant population-level impacts from wind energy development (Johnson and Erickson 2011).

A number of studies have attempted to document marbled murrelet activity patterns in wind energy development sites (Cooper and Sanzenbacher 2006, Nations and Erickson 2009). Using these activity patterns to predict potential fatalities and the population-level impacts of such fatalities is complex (Nations and Erickson 2009, Nelson et al. 2009). At the Radar Ridge wind energy development site in Washington, Nations and Erickson (2009) used a wind turbine collision model to predict that large wind turbines, operating continuously, would result in annual fatalities of 0.74 marbled murrelets per year, leading them to conclude that fatalities over the life of the project were expected to be low. In contrast, Nelson et al. (2009) examined the available data on marbled murrelet use at the site and concluded that the project was likely to have an adverse effect on marbled murrelets. Part of the uncertainty in predicting mortality rates stems from collision models with incomplete knowledge of bird behavior. Without site-specific and species-specific information on birds' avoidance behaviors, the ability to estimate mortality rates through collision models may be limited (Chamberlain et al. 2006).

Site topography and characteristics—A site's topography and ecological features often determine bird use, and may also directly influence collision mortality. For example, in a review of technical reports, Drewitt and Langston (2006) suggested that birds' responses to topography may include soaring along ridges or lowering flight height when along the coast or when crossing a ridge, which then increases collisions. Placing wind energy facilities in areas commonly used by raptors, such as slopes of hills or ridges, is thought to increase mortalities (Kuvlesky et al. 2007), although these are also the areas with the greatest wind resources. In Spain, high raptor morality resulted after wind energy facilities were constructed along a topographic bottleneck, an area where migrating birds are funneled by the surrounding landscape (e.g., mountains, rising winds) (Barrios and Rodriguez 2004). For migratory birds, available evidence suggests that birds migrate at relatively high elevations (above turbines), but may be vulnerable when at lower elevations owing to weather or when landing or taking off (Arnett et al. 2007, National Research Council 2007). In general, the effect of topography on bird migration remains poorly understood (Arnett et al. 2007, National Research Council 2007).

Researchers are also interested in how the layout design of the wind energy facility may also influence mortality within a site (Kuvlesky et al. 2007), but it is challenging to study different turbine configurations in well-designed comparisons, and there has been relatively little research on turbine configuration. Studies have found that mortalities may be concentrated in space within wind energy facilities, or may be more evenly distributed (e.g., Barrios and Rodriguez 2004). Researchers propose that variation in spatial pattern of mortalities results both from topographic features and variation in species behavior (Barrios and Rodriguez 2004). Ecological modifications of the site after construction will also influence direct mortality. For example, raptor populations may have increased in some cases around wind energy facilities because habitat alterations increased prey populations, ultimately leading to more collisions (Smallwood et al. 2007).

Turbine characteristics—Researchers have suggested that characteristics of the turbine, such as turbine height, structure, blade length, and lighting, may determine wildlife mortality (Kuvlesky et al. 2007), but results thus far show relatively limited impacts of turbine features. In a review of more than 30 studies from wind energy facilities (many of them unpublished reports), Barclay et al. (2007) found that the size of the rotor-swept area did not alter mortality rates, and that the per-turbine fatality rate for birds remained constant with increasing height. Although turbines are increasing in size, in many cases, migrating birds still tend to pass at higher elevations (Johnson and Erickson 2011), unless weather conditions and topographical conditions combine to lower birds' flying elevations (National Research Council 2007). Older style "lattice" type towers have been largely replaced by tubular towers to discourage birds from perching on towers, although some studies show no significant differences in mortality between lattice and tubular towers (Barrios and Rodriguez 2004, Smallwood et al. 2007). Lighting on turbines and other structures has been discussed as a factor increasing bird mortality among nighttime migrants since the 1950s, but recent research suggests that wind towers with flashing lights have low mortalities of migrants in comparison to communication towers, which are generally taller, often lit with some steady (nonflashing) lights, and have more infrastructure in the form of guy wires to support towers (Gehring et al. 2009, 2011; Kerlinger et al. 2010). Research from communication towers showed that steady burning (nonflashing) lights increase mortalities (Gehring et al. 2009), so researchers have recommended that only flashing lights be used in wind turbine sites (Kerlinger et al. 2010). A meta-analysis of technical reports from wind energy facilities found no significant difference in mortalities among turbines lit with flashing lights and those that are not lit (not all turbines in a wind energy facility are lit depending on their physical spacing) (Kerlinger et al. 2010). Recommendations and more specific information on lighting are included in federal and state guidelines (table 1).

Bird behavior—Turbine collisions are fundamentally a behavioral issue, with species' different tolerances of turbines leading to variable mortality rates among species. Researchers have documented a number of ways in which species' behavior alters their risk of collision mortality. Birds' vulnerabilities to collision are often linked to species-specific flight behavior (Barrios and Rodriguez 2004, de Lucas et al. 2008, Drewitt and Langston 2006). As discussed above, weather conditions and topography may alter bird behavior, and lead to collisions. Bird activity may also differ between sex and age, leading to different collision mortalities for different subgroups of a population (e.g., Stienen et al. 2008). Bird mortality rates often differ seasonally (e,g., most passerine fatalities in North America occur between April and October) (Arnett et al. 2007). Seasonal variation in fatalities appear to result from seasonal variations in bird populations, behavior, and migration activity, as well as variation in weather (e.g., Barrios and Rodriguez 2004, Osborn et al. 1998).

While it is unclear why species approach, or do not avoid, turbines, these avoidance rates are critical to better understand and predict avian mortality. Models that attempt to estimate collision risk by combining information on the structure and operation of turbines with bird size and flight show that small variations in avoidance rates (often estimated as greater than 0.95 in case studies) lead to relatively large increases in predicted collisions (Chamberlain et al. 2006). Because avoidance rates are often calculated based on the number of mortalities observed divided by the number of birds flying through the turbines' rotor-swept area, these rates may be subject to observer error and challenges of surveying bird behavior at high elevations at wind energy sites (Chamberlain et al. 2006).

Bats—

The impact of wind turbines on bats has increasingly been studied in North America over the past 5 to 10 years, spurred by reports of substantial bat mortalities from the mid-Atlantic highlands (Maryland, Pennsylvania, Virginia, and West Virginia). For example, one of the earliest studied facilities, the Mountaineer Wind Energy Center in West Virginia, had an estimated 1,400 to 4,000 bat deaths annually (>30 fatalities $MW^{-1} \cdot year^{-1}$) (Arnett et al. 2008). Substantial bat fatalities have also been reported in the Southeast and Midwest (Arnett et al. 2008, Kunz et al. 2007b), and bat fatalities may outnumber bird fatalities in some areas by 10 to 1 (Barclay et al. 2007). Arnett et al. (2008) reviewed 21 studies (some peer-reviewed) from 19 different wind energy facilities across the United States and Canada and found that tree-roosting species accounted for 75 percent of documented fatalities, with hoary bats (*Lasiurus cinereus*) comprising half of all fatalities (Arnett et al. 2008). Tree-roosting species are also referred to as migratory species: hibernation alone may not be sufficient to allow these bats to survive cold winters, and so they undertake long-distance migration to warmer climates where hibernation in trees is more likely to be successful (Popa-Lisseanu and Voigt 2009). Although background information on bat populations and activity is often lacking, evidence thus far suggests that the species composition of wind turbine mortality does not directly correspond to species' abundance at sites (Cryan and Barclay 2009, Jain et al. 2011).

Fatalities among bats occur as a result of direct collisions with rotor blades, and potentially as the result of barotrauma, the injuries caused when the motion of

While it is unclear why species approach, or do not avoid, turbines, these avoidance rates are critical to better understand and predict avian mortality. Models that attempt to estimate collision risk by combining information on the structure and operation of turbines with bird size and flight show that small variations in avoidance rates lead to relatively large increases in predicted collisions.

turbine blades causes rapid air pressure reduction. Blade tips in modern turbines rotate at speeds of 55 to 80 m/s, creating pressure drops of 5 to 10 kilopascals, which is sufficient to cause significant damage in mammals (Baerwald et al. 2008). Birds do not appear to suffer from barotrauma, likely because they have compact, rigid lungs and stronger pulmonary capillaries (Baerwald et al. 2008). The relative roles of barotrauma and other traumatic injury in causing mortality is an active area of investigation. At a wind energy facility in Alberta, Canada, up to 90 percent of bat fatalities showed internal hemorrhaging, but only half of all bat fatalities showed external injuries, leading authors to suggest that barotrauma is a significant cause of wind energy fatalities (Baerwald et al. 2008). However, a study from Wisconsin reported barotrauma and direct collisions were not always discernible (Grodsky et al. 2011) and Rollins et al. (2012) concluded that approximately 5 percent of wind energy mortalities could be attributed to barotrauma alone (using ruptured eardrums as the marker for barotrauma). Additional research on the relationship between collisions, pressure differentials, and mortalities will further refine our understanding of bat fatalities, but in this report, we consider the term collision or direct mortality to include physical injuries or fatalities resulting from interaction or proximity to turbines.

> **In the Pacific Northwest, little information exists on bat populations, migratory patterns, or wind energy facility impacts.**

In the Pacific Northwest, little information exists on bat populations, migratory patterns, or wind energy facility impacts. Forest-dwelling migratory species found in the region include the hoary bat and the silver-haired bat (*Lasionycteris noctivagan*). Other bat species present in the region include little brown myotis (*Myotis lucifugus*) and big brown bat (*Eptesicus fuscus*). At present there are no peer-reviewed studies examining the rates of bat mortality in Oregon and Washington, but Johnson and Erickson (2011) summarized technical reports on bat impacts in the Columbia Plateau region. They found bat mortality ranged from 0.27 bats/MW/year to 3.78/bats/MW/year (Young and Poulton 2009), which is lower than high mortalities reported in the East and upper Midwest (Arnett et al. 2008, Kunz et al. 2007b). Silver-haired and hoary bats made up nearly all of the fatalities (48 percent and 46 percent, respectively) (Johnson and Erickson 2011). Without more information on the relative abundance of different species prior to wind energy development, and the overall population abundance and distribution of bat species, it is challenging to evaluate the population-level impacts, or the cumulative effects of multiple wind-energy developments.

Site topography and characteristics—Among bats, no clear relationships between fatalities and habitat or topographic characteristics have been detected (Arnett et al. 2008, Stewart et al. 2007), although one recent study in Oklahoma found higher mortality rates concentrated at several turbines within a facility (Piorkowski and

O'Connell 2010). In this case, researchers suggested that mortality might result from a landscape feature (eroded ravine) serving as a conduit for daily movements of bats from a maternity colony (Piorkowski and O'Connell 2010). Otherwise, previous reviews have concluded that mortalities tended to be evenly distributed throughout wind energy facilities (Arnett et al. 2007, National Research Council 2007). There are concerns that wind energy facilities themselves modify habitat in a manner that attracts bats. The forest edges created by access roads may create hotspots of bat activity because edges enhance bat foraging for insects (Arnett et al. 2008, Stewart et al. 2007).

Turbine characteristics—Bat fatalities at wind energy facilities increase exponentially with wind turbine height, with the highest mortalities experienced with turbines taller than 65 m (Barclay et al. 2007). Within individual turbine sites, bats appear to be more active within the rotor-swept medium elevations than below the rotor blades, with bat sightings six times more common within rotor-swept areas (29 to 111 m) than below rotor blades (<29 m) (Horn et al. 2008). Although researchers have raised concerns about turbine lighting attracting insects and increasing bat collisions, lighting did not appear to affect the incidence of foraging bats around turbines in one study in West Virginia (Horn et al. 2008). A recent study suggested that certain turbine colors attracted more insects, in turn leading to a concentration of bats (Long et al. 2011).

Bat behavior—Behavioral responses to weather patterns and seasonal behavior are thought to play an important role in determining bat presence and fatalities (Cryan and Barclay 2009, Weller and Baldwin 2012). Collisions are a concern only when bats are active, generally from March or April through November for species that hibernate during the winter. However, tree-roosting species migrate to avoid cold weather, and in warmer climates, bats are more likely to be periodically active during the winter. Seasonally, the highest fatalities are reported during late summer and early fall when bats are migrating, with fewer fatalities during the spring migration (Kunz et al. 2007b). In general, low mortalities among bats have been documented during the summer maternity season, but the wind energy facilities studied were in open habitat such as cropland or shrub steppe, where forest-dwelling species are not expected to concentrate during maternity season (Arnett et al. 2008). A study of a wind energy facility adjacent to two large breeding colonies (2 million bats) of Brazilian free-tailed bats in Oklahoma found that over 80 percent of all bat mortalities were Brazilian free-tailed bats, and that approximately 60 percent of all bats killed were female, suggesting that bats in breeding colonies are vulnerable to wind energy facilities (Piorkowski and O'Connell 2010).

Within a site, bat activity may follow weather and insect activity. A study in southern California found that bats were more likely to be present at turbines when windspeeds were lower and temperatures higher, although including date and moon illumination also helped predict bat presence (Weller and Baldwin 2012). A study at the Mountaineer Wind Energy Facility in West Virginia found a significant correlation between insect and bat activity, suggesting that bats may be attracted to patches of insects (Horn et al. 2008). In this study, bat activity and fatalities peaked in the hours after sunset when insects were most active (Horn et al. 2008). Bat fatalities are also higher during periods of low windspeed, when insects are thought to be most active (Arnett et al. 2008). Weather patterns, such as low or heavy cloud cover, or thermal inversions, may cause bats to alter their flight patterns, increasing fatalities (Kunz et al. 2007b).

There have also been persistent questions about bat species' behavior and if bats show an attraction to wind turbines (Cryan and Barclay 2009). If bats' occurrence at wind energy facilities is coincidental, meaning fatalities occur where bat populations and turbines happen to overlap, populations might be more susceptible when migrating owing to migrants' clumped distribution or some other aspect of migratory behavior (e.g., flying higher than nonmigrants, or perhaps migrating bats are less likely to echolocate) (Cryan and Barclay 2009). In contrast, researchers have suggested that a number of wind energy facility features may attract bats. At wind energy facility sites, bats have been observed investigating the turbines, and alighting on turbines and monopoles (Horn et al. 2008). In one behavioral study, researchers documented that bats were struck by turbines during foraging and exploratory behavior, not as a result of straight-line flight through the wind facility (Horn et al. 2008). Lights, the sound of moving turbines, the motion of turbine blades, novel vegetation such as forest edges created by turbines or roads, insect aggregations that occur around wind energy facilities, or an attraction to turbines as potential roosts, mating, or gathering sites have all been suggested as factors that may attract bats to wind energy facilities (Cryan and Barclay 2009).

Best Management Practices to Minimize Effects of Wind Energy Facilities on Wildlife

Federal laws that pertain to wind energy and wildlife issues include the Migratory Bird Treaty Act, Bald and Golden Eagle Protection Act, Endangered Species Act, and National Environmental Policy Act, as well as relevant sections of the Clean Water Act and the use of aircraft warning lights as required by the Federal Aviation Administration (Arnett et al. 2007). Given concerns about wildlife habitat loss and direct mortality, there have been a number of efforts to expand beyond the current regulation and develop voluntary guidelines and best management practices for wind energy development. The USFWS land-based wind energy guidelines are the main national source for voluntary guidelines to help developers collect information, quantify the possible risks of wind energy projects to species of concern and their habitats, and evaluate these risks to make siting, construction, and operation decisions (U.S. Fish and Wildlife Service 2012). These are the primary guidelines for wind energy developers on federal and private land, and are intended to complement other federal law and policy that directs the siting and development of wind energy projects on federal lands.

The USFWS guidelines emerged over time, with an interim set of guidelines issued in 2003. Following public comment on the 2003 guidelines, the Secretary of the Interior created the Wind Turbine Guidelines Advisory Committee under the Federal Advisory Committee Act. This committee worked for more than 2 years to submit final recommendations to the Secretary of the Interior on March 4, 2010 (U.S. Fish and Wildlife Service 2011c). An internal working group at USFWS then used these recommendations to develop the USFWS draft land-based wind energy guidelines, which underwent two revisions: the first draft was released February 8, 2011, for a 90-day public comment period, and the second revision was released July 12, 2011, for a 21-day public comment period. Final guidelines were released in March 23, 2012. Our discussion below is based on the final guidelines.

The guidelines are intended to "promote compliance with relevant wildlife laws and regulations; encourage scientifically rigorous survey, monitoring, assessment, and research designs proportionate to the risk to species of concern; produce potentially comparable data across the Nation; mitigate, including avoid, minimize, and compensate for potential adverse effects on species of concern and their habitats; and improve the ability to predict and resolve effects locally, regionally, and nationally" (U.S. Fish and Wildlife Service 2012, p. 1). Guidelines are voluntary, and although individuals and companies cannot be absolved of their responsibilities under the Migratory Bird Treaty Act and Bald and Golden Eagle Protection Act, the USFWS does regard "a developer's or operator's adherence to these guidelines, including communication with the Service, as appropriate means of identifying and implementing reasonable and effective measures to avoid the take of species protected under the Migratory Bird Treaty Act and Bald and Golden Eagle Protection Act" (U.S. Fish and Wildlife Service 2012, p. 6).

The USFWS guidelines rely upon a tiered approach to iteratively evaluate risks and minimize the effects of a wind energy development project to fish, wildlife and their habitats, through an adaptive management framework. The first three tiers deal with site selection and planning and the last two with postconstruction monitoring and research:

The USFWS land-based wind energy guidelines are the main national source for voluntary guidelines to help developers collect information, quantify the possible risks of wind energy projects to species of concern and their habitats, and evaluate these risks to make siting, construction, and operation decisions.

Tier 1–Preliminary site evaluation (landscape-scale screening of potential sites)

Tier 2–Site characterization (broad characterization of one or more potential project sites)

Tier 3–Field studies to document site wildlife and habitat and predict project impacts

Tier 4–Postconstruction studies to estimate impacts

Tier 5–Other postconstruction studies and research

Early communication and use of these guidelines during a wind project's development is intended to ensure the greatest range of development and mitigation options. As a project progresses through these tiers, developers will formulate a Bird and Bat Conservation Strategy, to explain their studies, analyses, and reasoning while moving through tiers. The USFWS recommends that projects already under development or in operation implement those portions of the guidelines relevant to the current phases of the project. Projects that are already operational are therefore advised to confer with the USFWS about the postconstruction monitoring and research tiers (U.S. Fish and Wildlife Service 2012, p. 4). The tiered approach is described in the guidelines as a system to "lead to the appropriate amount of evaluation in proportion to the anticipated level of risk that a project may pose to species of concern and their habitats" (U.S. Fish and Wildlife Service 2012, p. 6). Study plans and the duration and intensity of study efforts should be tailored specifically for each unique site and the potential for significant adverse impacts on species of concern and their habitats (U.S. Fish and Wildlife Service 2012, p. 6).

In addition to the wind energy guidelines, USFWS released draft guidelines to reduce the impacts of wind development on eagles (U.S. Fish and Wildlife Service 2011a). Draft eagle guidelines provide "a national framework for assessing and mitigating risk specific to eagles through development of eagle conservation plans and issuance of programmatic incidental takes of eagles at wind turbine facilities" (U.S. Fish and Wildlife Service 2012, p. 3). These eagle guidelines are intended to be used in concert with the broader USFWS guidelines. We focus on these more general land-based wind energy guidelines (U.S. Fish and Wildlife Service 2012) to provide a comprehensive overview of guidelines and best management practices recommended by USFWS, but eagle guidelines provide more specific information for developers. The final Eagle Conservation Plan guidance will be released to the public through the USFWS Web site.

Other federal and state agencies have also developed guidelines and best management practices. The BLM underwent a large-scale planning process that issued wind energy best management guidelines through a record of decision in

2005 (USDI BLM 2005b). These guidelines are general in scope, with site-specific planning processes intended to further consider site configuration, monitoring program requirements, and appropriate mitigation measures (USDI BLM 2005). Forest Service directives are laid out in two documents, one dealing with wind energy siting and permitting, and a separate document dealing with wildlife monitoring at wind energy sites (USDA Forest Service 2011a, 2011b). These directives closely follow past literature, BLM's guidelines, as well as USFWS guidelines, and refer readers to these other references throughout the directives. Lastly, Oregon and Washington also have voluntary guidelines with content similar to the national USFWS guidelines, which may also be of interest to land managers in the Pacific Northwest. Below, we present the federal and state recommendations for each phase of a wind energy facility development: site selection and preparation, construction and operation practices, and postconstruction monitoring. We also present a summary of best management practices, with each practice listed under the potential threat (habitat loss or direct mortality), cross-referenced to the relevant scientific literature (table 1).

Site Selection

The primary management strategy to avoid or minimize the effects of habitat loss and direct collisions is to place wind energy facilities away from species of concern and areas of high wildlife value. The federal guidelines and those for Oregon and Washington all emphasize the best placement of wind turbines as the primary method to protect wildlife (Oregon Columbia Plateau Ecoregion Wind Energy Taskforce 2008, U.S. Fish and Wildlife Service 2012, USDA Forest Service 2011a, USDI BLM 2005b, Washington Department of Fish and Wildlife 2009).

In USFWS guidelines, Tier 1, or preliminary evaluation/screening of potential sites, is described as the stage when developers first examine a broad geographic area and conduct a preliminary evaluation of the general ecological context of a potential site or sites. Developers are encouraged to work with the USFWS during Tier 1, with this assessment also serving as preparation for future work with federal, state, tribal, and other local agencies. This first screening process allows developers to identify areas of high sensitivity due to "the presence of: 1) large blocks of intact native landscapes; 2) intact ecological communities; 3) fragmentation sensitive species' habitats; or 4) other important landscape-scale wildlife values" (U.S. Fish and Wildlife Service 2012, p. 12). With this information from Tier 1 collected, developers will have important information about the sensitivity of the site within a larger landscape context, early in the development process. This information can help

The primary management strategy to avoid or minimize the effects of habitat loss and direct collisions is to place wind energy facilities away from species of concern and areas of high wildlife value. The federal guidelines and those for Oregon and Washington all emphasize the best placement of wind turbines as the primary method to protect wildlife.

direct development away from locations that are associated with additional study need, greater mitigation requirements, and uncertainty. Alternatively, it can be used to identify the sensitive resources that will require further study if the site is to be developed "without significant adverse impacts to species of concern or local population(s)" (U.S. Fish and Wildlife Service 2012, p. 12). The guidelines note that some areas may be inappropriate for large-scale development because "they have been recognized according to scientifically credible information as having high wildlife value, based solely on their ecological rarity and intactness (e.g., Audubon Important Bird Areas, The Nature Conservancy portfolio sites, state wildlife action plan priority habitats)" (U.S. Fish and Wildlife Service 2012, p. 12). The USFWS guidelines include several suggested questions for developers under Tier 1:

1. Are there species of concern present on the proposed site(s), or is habitat (including designated critical habitat) present for these species?

2. Does the landscape contain areas where development is precluded by law or areas designated as sensitive according to scientifically credible information? Examples of designated areas include, but are not limited to: federally-designated critical habitat; high-priority conservation areas for non-government organizations (NGOs); or other local, state, regional, federal, tribal, or international categorizations.

3. Are there known critical areas of wildlife congregation, including, but not limited to: maternity roosts, hibernacula, staging areas, winter ranges, nesting sites, migration stopovers or corridors, leks, or other areas of seasonal importance?

4. Are there large areas of intact habitat with the potential for fragmentation, with respect to species of habitat fragmentation concern needing large contiguous blocks of habitat? (U.S. Fish and Wildlife Service 2012, p. 13).

The guidelines then outline a decision process, so that if answers to all of the four questions above are "no" for one or more sites found within the area of investigation, the assessment indicates a low probability of significant adverse effects to wildlife. In this case, the developer would then proceed to Tier 2 investigation of the site characteristics. However, if any of these questions is answered "yes," developers should proceed to Tier 2 to further assess the probability of significant adverse impacts to wildlife. Developers may consider abandoning the area or identifying ways in which project modifications will avoid or minimize potential significant adverse impacts (U.S. Fish and Wildlife Service 2012, p. 13). Within the Pacific Northwest, federal land management agencies are interested in conducting such a Tier 1 evaluation to guide prospective development. The BLM is conducting wildlife assessments for each state, examining areas where high-priority wildlife or habitats occur.[6] The wider scientific literature reveals increasing interest in large-scale assessments of wind energy development impacts. For example, researchers used species-distribution and habitat suitability modeling to map predicted habitat quality for the lesser prairie-chicken (*Tympanuchus pallidicinctus*) throughout western Kansas (Jarnevich and Laubhan 2011). Researchers hope these relatively coarse-scale models can help guide energy development away from prime prarie-chicken habitat (Jarnevich and Laubhan 2011). Other regional-scale models have also incorporated wind potential, to balance tradeoffs between species protection and energy development (Eichhorn and Drechsler 2010). The USFWS maintains a list of risk assessment tools, which may also be used during site characterization (U.S. Fish and Wildlife Service 2011b).

Following the USFWS guidelines, once a specific site of interest is selected on a landscape, the Tier 2 process allows developers and managers to look at more site-specific resources, and those that occur on smaller scales. During Tier 2, developers combine existing information with at least one site visit to complete their assessment. Questions posed to developers in the guidelines in Tier 2 are very similar the same questions posed in Tier 1, but are now applied to the site under consideration, with additional questions about plant communities, birds, and bats at the site (for more detail, see U.S. Fish and Wildlife Service 2012, p. 15). When completed, Tier 2 site characterizations are expected to generally contain three components: (1) a review of existing information including published or available literature, databases and maps of topography, land use and land cover, potential wetlands, wildlife, habitat, and sensitive plant distributions; (2) information gathered from agencies and organizations that have relevant scientific information to further help identify if there are bird, bat, or other wildlife issues; and (3) one or more reconnaissance-level site visits to evaluate current vegetation/habitat coverage and land management/ use (to help determine the baseline against which potential effects from the project would be evaluated) (U.S. Fish and Wildlife Service 2012, p. 15). More detail on Tier 2 and specific resources for assessments, including a framework for evaluating habitat fragmentation, are in the USFWS guidelines (U.S. Fish and Wildlife Service 2012, p. 15). Unless sufficient information is available to answer all Tier 2 questions and conclude either that a low probability of significant adverse impact to wildlife or that significant adverse impacts to species of concern cannot be adequately

---

[6] Buckner, G. 2010. Personal communication. Oregon state wildlife biologist, USDI Bureau of Land Management, 333 SW 1st Avenue, Portland, OR 97204.

mitigated, developers will proceed to Tier 3 to further consider potential impacts and mitigation.

Guidelines from BLM, Oregon, and Washington, and the Forest Service directives are all similar to USFWS guidelines in that they also recommend that developers avoid critical areas for wildlife, habitats of interest, or intact habitat. Forest Service guidelines list a number of siting considerations for species of management concern (defined as federally listed threatened and endangered species; species that are candidates for listing as threatened or endangered; Forest Service sensitive species, species of high public interest and state-protected species). For these species, directives advise potential project developers to:

1. Locate METs [meteorological towers], roads, turbines, and other necessary facilities away from protected areas or where ecological resources are known to be sensitive to human activities. Examples of these areas include wetlands, riparian zones, streams, lakes, bogs, or fens; globally unique, rare or threatened ecosystems; critical habitat of wildlife protected under Federal or State law; nests of hawks, eagle, falcons, and owls; and prairie or shrub-steppe grouse breeding grounds and habitat fragmentation.

2. Avoid or minimize the placement of towers and turbines in areas with a high incidence of frontal weather events that lead to frequent fog or mist if existing information indicates a high risk to migratory birds or bats during these weather events.

3. Avoid or minimize the placement of turbines in areas where topography and landscape features may funnel nocturnal migrants, such as over mountain passes, along river corridors, or ridge tops.

4. Use existing roads and utility corridors to the extent feasible, and minimize the number, length, and size of new roads, lay-down areas, and borrow areas.

5. Avoid placement of towers in habitat, security areas or critical range of species of management concern (USDA Forest Service 2011a, p. 11).

More detailed guidance on avoiding or minimizing the potential for collisions and disturbance through siting is provided throughout the document (USDA Forest Service 2011a).

In both Oregon and Washington state guidelines, developers are advised to develop wind energy facilities on agricultural or disturbed lands, use existing transmission corridors and road networks, or place transmission corridors and other linear facilities in disturbed lands. Forest Service directives, BLM guidelines, and

Washington state guidelines do not have an explicit staged or tiered process but do require preproject assessment to help design the project to avoid and minimize impacts to habitat and wildlife, followed by operational monitoring. Oregon state guidelines lead developers through five sequential phases, the first three of which deal with wind energy siting:

1. Macrositing to identify conflicts that may make a wind project prohibitively difficult to permit.
2. Preproject assessment to identify wildlife and habitat resources on the potential wind project site and micrositing corridors that will be used to locate specific turbines and associated infrastructure.
3. Micrositing to determine the final wind project design (i.e., the final placement of turbines, roads, transmission lines, and other wind project features).
4. Construction where protective measures are used to avoid and minimize impacts to wildlife.
5. Operational monitoring determines the actual direct mortality impacts of the wind project on wildlife.

Preconstruction Wildlife Surveys

Because wind energy facilities are a relatively new land use, and much of their impact depends upon the combination of the site characteristics, wind energy facility characteristics, and needs and responses of wildlife populations, monitoring wildlife populations is key to determine and mitigate wind energy facility impacts. Therefore all guidelines contain recommendations for surveys, before a wind energy facility is built, to determine wildlife habitat and use and anticipate direct mortality impacts.

Among existing guidelines, USFWS guidelines provide the most detailed recommendations about preconstruction survey methodology, intensity, and duration. Information on preconstruction wildlife monitoring is considered Tier 3 in the USFWS guidelines. Tier 3 recommends that developers study and further evaluate wildlife populations at a site in order to: "further evaluate a site for determining whether the wind energy project should be developed or abandoned; design and operate a site to avoid or minimize significant adverse impacts if a decision is made to develop; design compensatory mitigation measures if significant adverse habitat impacts cannot acceptably be avoided or minimized; determine duration and level of effort of postconstruction monitoring" (U.S. Fish and Wildlife Service 2012, p. 19). Guidelines state that protocols for monitoring will differ with the species or ecological community studied, and with the site characteristics. Some species may

Because wind energy facilities are a relatively new land use, and much of their impact depends upon the combination of the site characteristics, wind energy facility characteristics, and needs and responses of wildlife populations, monitoring wildlife populations is key to determine and mitigate wind energy facility impacts.

have specific protocols required by local, state, or federal agencies. Because of the need for flexibility and the variation that may be encountered between projects, there are no specific recommendations on protocol in the USFWS guidelines. However, guidelines do recommend that preconstruction surveys be sufficient to answer the following questions about a wind energy facility's potential impacts:

1. Do field studies indicate that species of concern are present on or likely to use the proposed site?

2. Do field studies indicate the potential for significant adverse impacts on the affected population of the species of habitat fragmentation concern?

3. What is the distribution, relative abundance, behavior, and site use of species of concern identified in Tiers 1 or 2, and to what extent do these factors expose these species to risk from the proposed wind energy project?

4. What are the potential risks of adverse impacts of the proposed wind energy project to individuals and local populations of species of concern or their habitats? (In the case of rare or endangered species, what are the possible impacts to such species and their habitats?)

5. How can developers mitigate identified significant adverse impacts?

6. Are there studies that should be initiated at this stage that would be continued in post-construction?" (U.S. Fish and Wildlife Service 2012, p. 20).

Comparing the efficacy of different survey techniques used in preconstruction monitoring is outside the scope of this document, but the USFWS guidelines provide more detailed information on monitoring and study for different species groups for each question above (U.S. Fish and Wildlife Service 2012). Guidelines also list additional references for methods and metrics tools in appendix C. As cited in the guidelines, Kunz et al. (2007a) discuss techniques for surveying nocturnal animals at length, and Strickland et al. (2011) overview methods and metrics for a range of taxa. U.S. Fish and Wildlife Service guidelines acknowledge the challenges of conducting surveys (often limited by cost), to support long-duration projects (30 years of operations). To accurately characterize site use and conditions, they state that preconstruction studies may need to occur over multiple years. There are no specific recommendations for survey duration, but guidelines advise that survey duration be determined by conditions at each site:

"The level of risk and the question of data requirements will be based on site sensitivity, affected species, and the availability of data from other sources. Accordingly, decisions regarding the studies should consider information gathered during the previous tiers, variability within and between seasons, and years where variability is likely to substantially affect answers to the Tier 3 questions. These studies should also be designed to collect data during relevant breeding, feeding, sheltering, staging, or migration periods for each species being studied. Additionally, consideration for the frequency and intensity of preconstruction monitoring should be site-specific and determined through consultation with an expert authority based on their knowledge of the specific species, level of risk and other variables present at each individual site" (U.S. Fish and Wildlife Service 2012, p. 25).

Forest Service directives, and Oregon and Washington state guidelines all include recommendations for survey duration. Forest Service directives require a monitoring plan that describes all pre- and postconstruction monitoring in order to obtain a permit for construction and operation of a wind energy facility. Complete information on monitoring plans and techniques are provided in the Forest Service Handbook (USDA Forest Service 2011b). Preconstruction monitoring must be conducted for a minimum of 2 years, and be sufficient to capture interannual and interseasonal variability, and can be extended:

"Preconstruction monitoring should occur across multiple seasons in order to evaluate interseasonal variability in habitat use and to sample during migration periods of the target species. The sample size within each season should be sufficient to detect differences in presence, abundance, or activity level between seasons. The sample size should also be sufficient to meet the monitoring objective (has the wind energy facility resulted in changes in presence, abundance, or activity level) with a reasonable level of confidence" (USDA Forest Service 2011b, p. 8).

Directives provide more detailed guidance on the wildlife response to measure (wildlife presence, abundance, or activity level) (USDA Forest Service 2011b, p. 8). Forest Service directives also recommend that monitoring include those factors that potentially are changed by wind energy development, and impact wildlife populations, such as habitat quality or quantity, habitat fragmentation, noise, road density, and traffic volume (USDA Forest Service 2011b, p. 7). To accurately assess the effects of wind energy development, guidelines recommend the use of a before-after-control-impact study, which examines both a wind energy facility site and an ecologically similar nondeveloped site before and after a wind energy facility is established, to separate management impacts from other ecological impacts. Information from preconstruction monitoring can be used in an adaptive management framework to design wind energy facilities (turbine location and configuration) to reduce potential impacts to wildlife (USDA Forest Service 2011b).

Oregon guidelines recommend 1 full year of raptor nest surveys and 1 year of avian use surveys, as well as bat surveys and surveys for threatened and endangered species and additional species of concern, if necessary. Survey durations may be reduced if there is preexisting relevant data, or expanded if managers expect high wildlife use of the wind energy facility site, if there is little background data, or if the project is especially large or complex. Washington's guidelines recommend at a minimum 1 full year of avian use surveys, and one raptor nest survey. The surveys are to be taken during the breeding season within 1.6 km (1 mile) of the project to determine potential impacts of construction, with a larger survey area (e.g., a 3.2-km [2-mile] buffer around project site) recommended if there is some likelihood of the occurrence of nesting state and federally threatened and endangered raptor species. Two or more years of relevant data are recommended if (1) risk to avian groups of concern is estimated to be high, (2) there is limited or no relevant data regarding seasonal use of the project site (e.g., data from nearby areas of similar habitat type), and (3) the project is significantly diverse in habitat and species. The BLM guidelines do not specify duration for preconstruction surveys.

Construction and Operation Practices

When the decision to proceed with a project has been made, there are a number of specific best management practices for the operation and design of the wind energy facility discussed in different guidelines, including factors such as lighting and vehicle operation (table 1). There are also some recent developments in the scientific literature that focus on how to best manage the time turbines are active. Although research has not yet yielded a recognized suite of best practices for managing turbine operation to reduce wildlife collisions, we summarize available information below.

Strategies for modifying turbine operation may focus on particular times or weather conditions when wildlife is thought to be most active. For example, research indicates that bats are most active in the 2 hours after sunset and that their activity is closely tied to weather patterns and daily changes in insect abundance, so that stopping turbine operation during these periods would likely decrease fatalities (Horn et al. 2008). Another strategy focuses on changing the minimum windspeed at which turbines begin to turn and generate electricity (termed a "cut-in speed") so that turbines remain idle at low windspeeds. This approach was successful in reducing bat mortality when tested in both Alberta, Canada and in the state of Pennsylvania in the United States (Arnett et al. 2011, Baerwald et al. 2009). In both instances, reductions in cut-in speed did not substantially reduce the amount of electricity generated because electricity is generated more efficiently at higher windspeeds, so that curtailing energy generation at lower speeds had a relatively small impact on total energy generated (Arnett et al. 2011, Baerwald et al. 2009). In addition, changes in cut-in speed occurred only at night when bats were active, allowing full energy production during the day.

These experiments suggest that revising operational timing can be done with a high level of precision by working with facility managers to target specific turbines under certain conditions. For raptors, researchers have suggested stopping turbines at the top of slopes when the weather conditions indicate the highest risk of collision (e.g., when winds are strong and facing perpendicularly to the slope) (Smallwood et al. 2009). Researchers are also experimenting with real-time systems that use radar information on bat and bird presence to curtail turbines only when animals are present (U.S. Fish and Wildlife Service 2012, p. 47). Changing cut-in speeds, or otherwise modifying turbine activity with weather patterns or wildlife activity, will need to be further studied to determine this technique's efficacy, but such targeted strategies are likely to be preferred over broader constrictions on operation. For example, a wind energy facility in West Virginia agreed to downscale a wind energy facility and stop operation completely during Indiana bat migration as part of a lawsuit settlement (turbines are operational only when bats are hibernating from mid-November to March 31) (Smith 2010).

Postconstruction Monitoring

After a wind energy facility becomes operational, current guidelines call for monitoring so that wind energy facility operation and impacts on wildlife can be assessed over time, in an adaptive management framework. In the USFWS's tiered system, postconstruction monitoring falls under Tier 4. Tier 4 includes monitoring both wildlife fatalities and other effects that result from project construction and operation. Guidelines recommend that postconstruction monitoring be designed to answer the following questions, related to fatalities and changes in habitat:

Fatality studies
1. "What are the bird and bat fatality rates for the project?"
2. "What are the fatality rates of species of concern?"
3. "How do the estimated fatality rates compare to the predicted fatality rates?"
4. "Do bird and bat fatalities vary within the project site in relation to site characteristics?"

5. "How do the fatality rates compare to the fatality rates from existing projects in similar landscapes with similar species composition and use?"
6. "What is the composition of fatalities in relation to migrating and resident birds and bats at the site?"
7. "Do fatality data suggest the need for measures to reduce impacts?" (U.S. Fish and Wildlife Service 2012, p. 35).

Habitat loss, degradation, and fragmentation

1. How do postconstruction habitat quality and spatial configuration of the study area compare to predictions for species of concern identified in Tier 3 studies?
2. Were any behavioral modifications or indirect impacts noted in regard to species of concern?
3. If significant adverse impacts were predicted for species of concern, and the project was altered to mitigate for adverse impacts, were those efforts successful?
4. If significant adverse impacts were predicted for species of concern, and the project was altered to mitigate for adverse impacts, were those efforts successful? (U.S. Fish and Wildlife Service 2012, p. 40).

Further information on postconstruction monitoring design and methods is included in the USFWS guidelines, including information on the duration and frequency of monitoring, number of turbines to monitor, delineation of carcass search plots, transects and habitat mapping, general search protocols, field bias and error assessment, and estimators of fatality (U.S. Fish and Wildlife Service 2012, p. 35–42). There are no fixed recommendations for postconstruction monitoring duration, but guidelines include survey decision-support matrixes that pair recommended duration and intensities of monitoring with perceived risk to wildlife identified in Tier 3, for both fatalities and habitat changes (U.S. Fish and Wildlife Service 2012, p. 39, 42).

Lastly, USFWS guidelines Tier 5: "Other postconstruction studies and research," describes the settings where additional research may be needed. The USFWS anticipates that Tier 5 will not be necessary for most wind energy projects because the tiered approach would steer projects away from sites where this additional, potentially complex and time-consuming work would be required. Guidelines propose the following questions to determine if research is needed (i.e., answering "yes" to any of these questions might indicate that a Tier 5 study is needed):

1. "To the extent that the observed fatalities exceed anticipated fatalities, are those fatalities potentially having a significant adverse impact on local populations? Are observed direct and indirect impacts to habitat having a significant adverse impact on local populations?"
2. "Were mitigation measures implemented (other than fee in lieu) not effective? This includes habitat mitigation measures as well as measures undertaken to reduce collision fatalities."
3. "Are the estimated impacts of the proposed project likely to lead to population declines in the species of concern (other than federally-listed species)?" (U.S. Fish and Wildlife Service 2012, p. 43).

More specific information about each of these questions and the circumstances in which Tier 5 studies may be conducted are provided in the USFWS guidelines, as well as some examples of Tier 5 studies.

Forest Service directives provide postconstruction monitoring guidance and require a minimum of 2 years of postconstruction monitoring, with an additional minimum of 1 year if any significant risks to species of management concern are identified (USDA Forest Service 2011b). An authorized officer can decide to require additional monitoring, based on the level of risk to species of management concern and the results of the first 2 years of monitoring. Directives state that long-term monitoring is essential to understanding the relationships between wildlife effects and the facility design and operation (USDA Forest Service 2011b, p. 9). More detailed information on postconstruction monitoring design and methods, including determining sample size, estimating mortality, monitoring tools, and evolving technology, is provided in Forest Service directives (USDA Forest Service 2011b). Information from postconstruction monitoring is intended to be used in an adaptive management framework, to refine operation of existing facilities, and guide development of future facilities (USDA Forest Service 2011b). Among state guidelines in the Pacific Northwest, Oregon provides specific guidance for survey duration (2 years of bird and bat fatality monitoring, with adjustment as determined with the management agency), while Washington requires developers to work with managers to determine the duration and scope of the monitoring (Oregon Columbia Plateau Ecoregion Wind Energy Taskforce 2008, Washington Department of Fish and Wildlife 2009). The BLM guidelines do not specify duration for postconstruction monitoring but state that "monitoring program requirements, including adaptive management strategies, shall be established at the project level to ensure that potential adverse impacts of wind energy development are mitigated" (USDI BLM 2005b, p. A7).

Future Research Needs for Minimizing Effects of Wind Energy Facilities on Wildlife

While there has been increasing scientific and management interest in understanding the impacts of wind energy on wildlife, many central questions about the relationship between wind energy facilities and wildlife populations remain unknown. Land managers require accurate information on the effects of wind energy facilities on wildlife, as supported by scientific studies, to formulate best management practices and manage wind energy developments. To further refine management and development of wind energy facilities, we draw from the research needs discussed in the scientific literature to synthesize priorities for future research.

General Research Needs

- Long-term, before-after-control-impact studies are needed. In the scientific literature, there are repeated calls for longer term, scientifically robust studies before and after wind energy facility establishment to truly understand their impacts on wildlife species and to effectively compare different sites (Carrete et al. 2009, Cryan and Barclay 2009, Kunz et al. 2007b, Kuvlesky et al. 2007, Masden et al. 2009a, Stewart et al. 2007). Researchers prefer the use of which examine both a wind energy facility site and a nondeveloped site before and after a wind energy facility is established to separate management impacts from other ecological impacts (Kuvlesky et al. 2007). Such studies require careful matching of developed and control sites to relate results to the effects of wind energy development.

- Collaboration and data sharing with the wind energy industry could enhance research. Turbine facilities are uniquely suited for experimentation in their operations (turbine speed, activity, and placement), so that cooperation with industry could lead to significant gains in understanding how facility design and operation affects wildlife (Cryan and Barclay 2009). In addition, the industry has collected substantial site-specific information on wildlife populations before and after wind energy facility establishment, but such information is not always publicly available. As interest in wind energy development continues on public lands, data sharing could enhance federal land managers' abilities to efficiently and accurately assess the potential effects of wind energy developments.

- Multisite studies will enhance scientific understanding. Studies involving multiple sites can provide more robust research results than studies carried out at one site, although larger studies take more time and resources (U.S. Fish and Wildlife Service 2012).

- Better methods to estimate population-level and cumulative impacts of wind energy facilities on wildlife. Understanding of behavioral responses or short-term effects of wind energy development are of limited use without expanded information on the population-level impact of habitat loss, disturbance, or mortality (Carrete et al. 2009, Masden et al. 2009a, Telleria 2009). Moving from a site-level impact to a population-level impact requires the ability to examine the cumulative impacts on wildlife populations, which will require information about species' populations and ecology across their ranges as well as population models to simulate different scenarios of habitat loss and heightened mortality (Kuvlesky et al. 2007). As wind energy facilities proliferate, there has been increasing concern about their cumulative impact. However, there is no clear source of funding for this fundamental, population-level research because wind energy developers conduct assessments at smaller scales, focused on specific development sites.

- For bats, large-scale population surveys and more ecological studies are needed. Because there are no large-scale population estimates or surveys of bat species (Kunz et al. 2007b, Weller et al. 2009), it is difficult to understand how wind energy facility impacts at a site affect larger populations. Bat ecology and population dynamics are poorly known, but a better understanding of bat ecology, population dynamics, and migration is key to understanding the impacts of wind energy facilities on bats (fig. 4). However, as stated above, obtaining funding for this fundamental research may be challenging.

Research Needs for Minimizing Habitat Loss or Modification

- How does wildlife respond to wind energy facilities, especially sage grouse and terrestrial mammals? There are limited studies of wildlife responses to wind energy facility developments, although previous studies on habitat loss and modification from road networks or other types of energy development may be helpful in predicting wildlife response to wind energy facilities. For sage grouse, the magnitude and proximal causes (e.g., noise, height of structures, movement, human activity, etc.) of those impacts on vital rates in grouse populations should be further studied (Becker et al. 2009). Information gained from such research should enhance our understanding of the buffer distances that are necessary to avoid or minimize adverse impacts of wind energy facilities on sage grouse. For both large and small mammals, there is little information on how species react to wind energy facilities and what kind of effects the loss and modification of habitat has on these species (Kuvlesky et al. 2007).

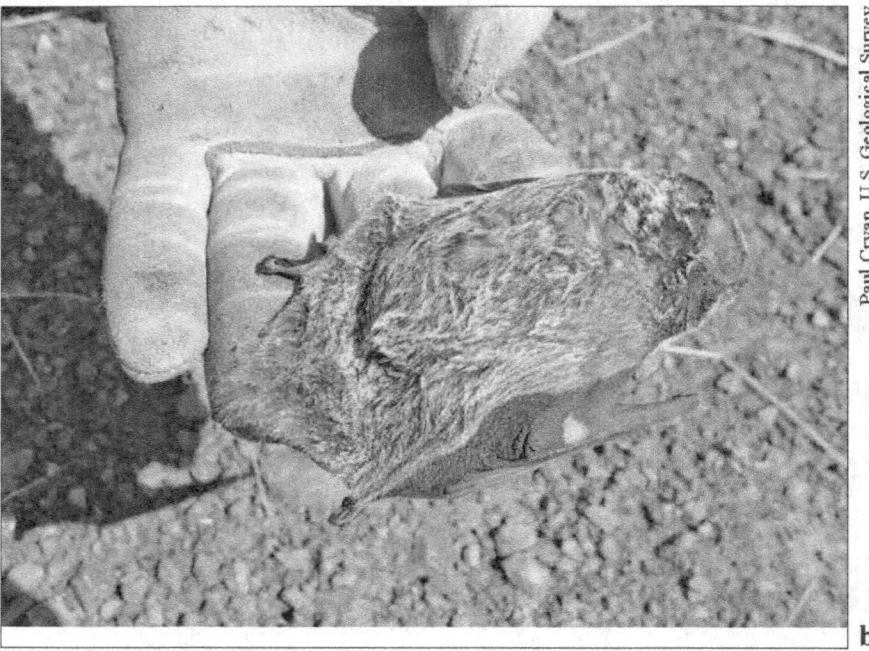

Figure 4—(a) A hoary bat roosting on the branch of a tree. (b) A hoary bat found dead beneath a wind turbine, an apparent victim of a blade strike or near-contact barotrauma.

- How does turbine noise affect wildlife? Noise effects of wind energy facilities have mostly been studied in people, but past research on wildlife and noise suggests that wind turbines may affect wildlife. Topics of future research may include how wind facilities affect background sound levels; whether masking, disturbance, and acoustical fragmentation occur; and how turbine operation, construction, and maintenance sound levels can differ by topographic area (U.S. Fish and Wildlife Service 2012, p. 46). Experimental research that can isolate noise from other features of wind energy development (e.g., examine the effects of turbine noise, visual disturbance caused by turbines, or traffic noise in isolation) will enhance our understanding of wind energy facility development and operation.

Research Needs for Minimizing Direct Mortality

- **Better methods to predict the impact of wind turbines are needed.** For both bats and birds, researchers would like to understand how weather, turbine design, and layout will relate to wildlife activity. Managers and researchers need better risk assessment models with appropriate confidence intervals on different scales to evaluate potential impacts of wind energy facilities. Refining efforts to predict collision risk and undertake regional assessments of wind energy facility impacts will help minimize impacts before facilities are constructed (Baisner et al. 2010).

- **Greater understanding of bat and bird migratory routes and behavior.** If bat collisions occur more frequently where bat populations are congregated, researchers will need a greater understanding of migratory behavior. Monitoring thus far has suggested that migratory bat species are most often those struck or injured by turbines. With a greater understanding of migratory patterns, wind energy facilities might be able to avoid migration routes or curtail wind energy facilities during active migration (Cryan and Barclay 2009). However, there is very little information on bat migratory patterns. Similarly, to better understand potential impacts of wind turbines on birds, researchers require better knowledge of migratory patterns and behavior for raptors and songbirds. Longer periods of pre and postconstruction monitoring will enhance our understanding of how bat activity and fatalities, in particular, relate to landscape conditions (topography, land cover) as well as weather conditions (e.g., windspeed, barometric pressure, air temperature), and the design of wind energy facilities (e.g., turbine size and height, the arrangement of turbines) (Arnett et al. 2008, Baldwind and Weller 2012, Kunz et al. 2007b).

- **Develop and refine techniques for monitoring nocturnal bird and bat behavior and activity.** Studies of bat and bird behavior pose significant logistical challenges: turbines can be as tall as 40-story buildings, and migratory routes can span continents (Cryan and Barclay 2009). There are many different monitoring methods for nocturnal animals, including radar, thermal imaging, and acoustic monitoring. Refining these types of monitoring while combining them with physiological analysis of carcasses (e.g., using stable isotopes to determine migratory patterns or studies of reproductive status to examine demography) may yield valuable insights into patterns of wildlife mortality (Kunz et al. 2007a).
- **Better knowledge of raptor behavior in relation to wind turbines.** Raptors are species of conservation concern, and understanding how site-specific raptor behavior combines with wind turbine design, configuration, activity, and weather to produce mortalities would be valuable for managers.
- **Behavioral research to examine why bats collide with turbines.** At present, researchers largely do not know if bat collisions with turbines are occurring coincidentally (i.e., collisions are higher where there is more bat activity) or if bats are attracted to turbines, resulting in more collisions (Cryan and Barclay 2009). Researchers also require better data to understand exactly how bats are interacting with turbines, and under what circumstances (weather, site characteristics, turbine design) they are injured/killed or escape injury (Horn et al. 2008). If bats are attracted to turbines, this preference would have significant implications for management, as managers might be able to minimize attractive features. Therefore, Cryan and Barclay (2009) recommended behavioral research to further examine this "attractive" turbine hypothesis as a top priority.
- **Further investigation into deterrents to decrease collisions.** To reduce collisions, researchers and managers would like to develop deterrents to increase turbine avoidance. No one effective deterrent has emerged from research thus far, but a number of acoustic deterrents have been used in experiments (U.S. Fish and Wildlife Service 2012, p. 47).

Conclusion

Both nationally and in the Pacific Northwest region (Oregon and Washington) there is growing public interest and policy pressure to develop wind energy facilities as a source of renewable energy. Wind energy facilities in the Pacific Northwest have expanded rapidly on private lands over the past decade, and there is now growing interest in development on federal lands. However, wind energy development has the potential to harm wildlife directly through collisions with wind turbines and transmission lines, as well as indirectly by modifying habitat. While information about the impacts of wind turbines on birds and bats has grown over the past decade, information on population-level effects over time as well as information on a wider range of species remains relatively unknown. Current federal and state guidelines acknowledge this uncertainty by emphasizing preconstruction studies, avoiding key wildlife habitat and species of concern when siting wind energy facilities, and conducting postconstruction monitoring of wind energy facility impacts. As wind energy development proceeds, augmenting this site-level research with basic research on key wildlife species' migration, demography, and populations will be helpful in enhancing our ability to predict and understand population-level and cumulative impacts of wind energy facilities on wildlife.

Acknowledgments

This work was supported by the Station Director's Office, Pacific Northwest Research Station. This report also served to fulfill the requirements, in part, of the Presidential Management Fellows Program for Miranda Mockrin. The document benefited from constructive reviews received from Ted Weller, Martin Raphael, and Dale Strickland. We also wish to thank Joyce Vandenbrook for her work creating a figure.

English Equivalents

When you know:	Multiply by:	To get:
Meters (m)	3.28	Feet
Kilometers (km)	.621	Miles
Hectares	2.47	Square feet
Square meters (m^2)	10.76	Acres
Kilopascals (Kpa)	.145038	Pounds per square inch

Literature Cited

74 CFR 46836. 2009. 50 CFR Parts 13 and 22. Eagle Permits; Take Necessary To Protect Interests in Particular Localities.

75 CFR 13910. 2010. 50 CFR Part 17 Endangered and Threatened Wildlife and Plants; 12-Month Findings for Petitions to List the Greater Sage Grouse (*Centrocercus urophasianus*) as Threatened or Endangered.

76 CFR 47354. 2011. Final Directives for Forest Service Wind Energy Special Use Authorizations, Forest Service Manual 2720, Forest Service Handbooks 2609.13 and 2709.11.

American Wind Energy Association. 2011. U.S. wind industry year-end 2010 market report. http://www.awea.org/learnabout/publications/loader. cfm?csModule=security/getfile&PageID=5083. (30 March 2011).

Arnett, E.; Inkley, D.; Johnson, D.; Larkin, R.; Manes, S.; Manville, A.; Mason, J.; Morrison, M.; Strickland, M.; Thresher, R. 2007. Impacts of wind energy facilities on wildlife and wildlife habitat. Wildlife Society Technical Review 07-2: 1–47.

Arnett, E.B.; Brown, W.K.; Erickson, W.P.; Fiedler, J.K.; Hamilton, B.L.; Henry, T.H.; Jain, A.; Johnson, G.D.; Kerns, J.; Koford, R.R. 2008. Patterns of bat fatalities at wind energy facilities in North America. Journal of Wildlife Management. 72: 61–78.

Arnett, E.B.; Huso, M.M.P.; Schirmacher, M.R.; Hayes, J.P. 2011. Altering turbine speed reduces bat mortality at wind-energy facilities. Frontiers in Ecology and the Environment. 9: 209–214.

Associated Press. 2009. Golden eagle killed by Washington wind turbines. Seattle Times. May 19. http://seattletimes.nwsource.com/html/localnews/2009237912_ apwawindturbineeagle1stldwritethru.html. (30 March 2011).

Avian Power Line Interaction Committee. 2006. Suggested practices for avian protection on power lines: state of the art in 2006. Washington, DC and Sacramento, CA: Edison Institute, California Energy Commission. 207 p.

Baerwald, E.F.; D'Amours, G.H.; Klug, B.J.; Barclay, R.M.R. 2008. Barotrauma is a significant cause of bat fatalities at wind turbines. Current Biology. 18: 695–696.

Baerwald, E.F.; Edworthy, J.; Holder, M.; Barclay, R.M.R. 2009. A large-scale mitigation experiment to reduce bat fatalities at wind energy facilities. Journal of Wildlife Management. 73: 1077–1081.

Baisner, A.J.; Andersen, J.L.; Findsen, A.; Yde Granath, S.W.; Madsen, K.Ø.; Desholm, M. 2010. Minimizing collision risk between migrating raptors and marine wind farms: development of a spatial planning tool. Environmental Management. 46: 1–8.

Barber, J.R.; Crooks, K.R.; Fristrup, K.M. 2010. The costs of chronic noise exposure for terrestrial organisms. Trends in Ecology and Evolution. 25: 180–189.

Barclay, R.M.R.; Baerwald, E.F.; Gruver, J.C. 2007. Variation in bat and bird fatalities at wind energy facilities: assessing the effects of rotor size and tower height. Canadian Journal of Zoology. 85: 381–387.

Barrios, L.; Rodriguez, A. 2004. Behavioural and environmental correlates of soaring-bird mortality at on-shore wind turbines. Journal of Applied Ecology. 41: 72–81.

Becker, J.M.; Tagestad, J.D.; Duberstein, C.A.; Downs, J.L. 2009. Sage-grouse and wind energy: biology, habits, and potential effects from development. PNNL-18567. Richland, WA: Pacific Northwest National Laboratory. 33 p.

Carrete, M.; Sanchez-Zapata, J.A.; Benitez, J.R.; Lobon, M.; Donazar, J.A. 2009. Large-scale risk-assessment of wind-farms on population viability of a globally endangered long-lived raptor. Biological Conservation. 142: 2954–2961.

Chamberlain, D.E.; Rehfisch, M.R.; Fox, A.D.; Desholm, M.; Anthony, S.J. 2006. The effect of avoidance rates on bird mortality predictions made by wind turbine collision risk models. Ibis. 148: 198–202.

Connelly, J.W.; Schroeder, M.A.; Sands, A.R.; Braun, C.E. 2000. Guidelines to manage sage grouse populations and their habitats. Wildlife Society Bulletin. 28: 967–985.

Cooper, B.A.; Sanzenbacher, B.A. 2006. A radar study of marbled murrelets at the proposed Bear River Windpark, California, Summer 2006. Forest Grove, OR: ABR, Inc. 15 p.

Cryan, P.M.; Barclay, R.M.R. 2009. Causes of bat fatalities at wind turbines: hypotheses and predictions. Journal of Mammalogy. 90: 1330–1340.

de Lucas, M.; Janss, G.F.E.; Whitfield, D.P.; Ferrer, M. 2008. Collision fatality of raptors in wind farms does not depend on raptor abundance. Journal of Ecology. 45: 1695–1703.

de Lucas, M.; Ferrer, M.; Bechard, M.J.; Muñoz, A.R. 2012. Griffon vulture mortality at wind farms in southern Spain: distribution of fatalities and active mitigation measures. Biological Conservation. 147: 184–189.

Dahl, E.L.; Bevanger, K.; Nygård, T.; Røskaft, E.; Stokke, B.G. 2012. Reduced breeding success in white-tailed eagles at Smøla windfarm, western Norway, is caused by mortality and displacement. Biological Conservation. 145: 79–85.

Drewitt, A.L.; Langston, R.H.W. 2006. Assessing the impacts of wind farms on birds. Ibis. 148: 29–42.

Eichhorn, M.; Drechsler, M. 2010. Spatial trade-offs between wind power production and bird collision avoidance in agricultural landscapes. Ecology and Society. 15: 10.

Executive Order No. 13514. 74 FR 52117, October 8, 2009.

Fahrig, L.; Rytwinski, T. 2009. Effects of roads on animal abundance: an empirical review and synthesis. Ecology and Society. 14(1): 21. http://www. ecologyandsociety.org/vol14/iss21/art21/. (30 March 2011).

Frick, W.F.; Pollock, J.F.; Hicks, A.C.; Langwig, K.E.; Reynolds, D.S.; Turner, G.G.; Butchkoski, C.M.; Kunz, T.H. 2010. An emerging disease causes regional population collapse of a common North American bat species. Science. 329: 679–682.

Garvin, J.C.; Jennelle, C.S.; Drake, D.; Grodsky, S.M. 2011. Response of raptors to a windfarm. Journal of Applied Ecology. 48: 199–209.

Gehring, J.; Kerlinger, P.; Manville, A.M. 2009. Communication towers, lights, and birds: successful methods of reducing the frequency of avian collisions. Ecological Applications. 19: 505–514.

Gehring, J.; Kerlinger, P.; Manville, I.; Albert, M. 2011. The role of tower height and guy wires on avian collisions with communication towers. The Journal of Wildlife Management. 75: 848–855.

Grodsky, S.M.; Behr, M.J.; Gendler, A.; Drake, D.; Dieterle, B.D.; Rudd, R.J.; Walrath, N.L. 2011. Investigating the causes of death for wind turbine-associated bat fatalities. Journal of Mammalogy. 92: 917–925.

Gucinski, H.; Furniss, M.J.; Ziemer, R.R.; Mh, B. 2001. Forest roads: a synthesis of scientific information. Gen. Tech. Rep. PNW-GTR-509. Portland, OR: U.S. Department of Agriculture, Forest Service, Pacific Northwest Research Station. 103 p.

Harju, S.M.; Dzialak, M.R.; Taylor, R.C.; Hayden-Wing, L.D.; Winstead, J.B. 2010. Thresholds and time lags in effects of energy development on greater sage-grouse populations. Journal of Wildlife Management. 74: 437–448.

Hessler, D.M.; Hessler, G.F. 2011. Recommended noise level design goals and limits at residential receptors for wind turbine developments in the United States. Noise Control Engineering Journal. 59: 94–104.

Holloran, M.J.; Kaiser, R.C.; Hubert, W.A. 2010. Yearling greater sage-grouse response to energy development in Wyoming. Journal of Wildlife Management. 74: 65–72.

Horn, J.W.; Arnett, E.B.; Kunz, T.H. 2008. Behavioral responses of bats to operating wind turbines. Journal of Wildlife Management. 72: 123–132.

Hunt, W.G. 2002. Golden eagles in a perilous landscape: predicting the effects of mitigation for wind turbine blade-strike mortality. Consultant report to California Energy Commission, Sacramento, California. Santa Cruz, CA. 52 p.

Jain, A.A.; Koford, R.R.; Hancock, A.W.; Zenner, G.G. 2011. Bat mortality and activity at a northern Iowa wind resource area. The American Midland Naturalist. 165: 185–200.

Jarnevich, C.S.; Laubhan, M.K. 2011. Balancing energy development and conservation: a method utilizing species distribution models. Environmental Management. 47: 926–936.

Johnson, G.D.; Erickson, W.P. 2011. Avian, bat, and habitat cumulative impacts associated with wind energy development in the Columbia Plateau Ecoregion of eastern Washington and Oregon. May 2011 updated report. Prepared for Klickitat County Planning Department. Western EcoSystems Technology, Inc. Cheyenne, WY. 39 p.

Johnson, G.D.; Erickson, W.P.; Strickland, M.D.; Shepherd, M.F.; Shepherd, D.A.; Sarappo, S.A. 2003. Mortality of bats at a large-scale wind power development at Buffalo Ridge, Minnesota. American Midland Naturalist. 150: 332–342.

Johnson, G.D.; Holloran, M.J. 2010. Greater sage-grouse and wind energy development: a review of the issues. Commissioned by Renewable Northwest Project. 80 p. http://west-inc.com/reports/FINAL%20RNP%20grouse%20 and%20wind%204-14-10.pdf. (30 March 2011).

Kerlinger, P.; Gehring, J.L.; Erickson, W.P.; Curry, R.; Jain, A.; Guarnaccia, J. 2010. Night migrant fatalities and obstruction lighting at wind turbines in North America. The Wilson Journal of Ornithology. 122: 744–754.

Knopper, L.D.; Ollson, C.A. 2011. Health effects and wind turbines: a review of the literature. Environmental Health. 10: 78.

Kunz, T.H.; Arnett, E.B.; Cooper, B.M.; Erickson, W.P.; Larkin, R.P.; Mabee, T.; Morrison, M.L.; Strickland, M.D.; Szewczak, J.M. 2007a. Assessing impacts of wind-energy development on nocturnally active birds and bats: a guidance document. Journal of Wildlife Management. 71: 2449–2486.

Kunz, T.H.; Arnett, E.B.; Erickson, W.P.; Hoar, A.R.; Johnson, G.D.; Larkin, R.P.; Strickland, M.D.; Thresher, R.W.; Tuttle, M.D. 2007b. Ecological impacts of wind energy development on bats: questions, research needs, and hypotheses. Frontiers in Ecology and the Environment. 5: 315–324.

Kuvlesky, W.P.; Brennan, L.A.; Morrison, M.L.; Boydston, K.K.; Ballard, B.M.; Bryant, F.C. 2007. Wind energy development and wildlife conservation: challenges and opportunities. Journal of Wildlife Management. 71: 2487–2498.

Leddy, K.L.; Higgins, K.F.; Naugle, D.E. 1999. Effects of wind turbines on upland nesting birds in Conservation Reserve Program grasslands. Wilson Bulletin. 111: 100–104.

Long, C.V.; Flint, J.A.; Lepper, P.A. 2011. Insect attraction to wind turbines: Does colour play a role? European Journal of Wildlife Research. 57: 323–331.

Longcore, T.; Rich, C.; Gauthreaux Jr, S.A. 2008. Height, guy wires, and steady-burning lights increase hazard of communication towers to nocturnal migrants: a review and meta-analysis. The Auk. 125: 485–492.

Madders, M.; Whitfield, D.P. 2006. Upland raptors and the assessment of wind farm impacts. Ibis. 148: 43–56.

Madsen, J.; Boertmann, D. 2008. Animal behavioral adaptation to changing landscapes: spring-staging geese habituate to wind farms. Landscape Ecology. 23: 1007–1011.

Manville, A.M., II. 2004. Prairie grouse leks and wind turbines: U.S. Fish and Wildlife Service justification for a 5-mile buffer from leks; additional grassland songbird recommendations (peer-reviewed briefing paper). Arlington, VA: Division of Migratory Bird Management. On file with: USFWS Division Migratory Bird Management, 4401 N. Fairfax Dr., Mailstop MBSP-4107, Arlington, VA 22203.

Masden, E.A.; Fox, A.D.; Furness, R.W.; Bullman, R.; Haydon, D.T. 2009a. Cumulative impact assessments and bird/wind farm interactions: Developing a conceptual framework. Environmental Impact Assessment Review. 30: 1–7.

Masden, E.A.; Haydon, D.T.; Fox, A.D.; Furness, R.W.; Bullman, R.; Desholm, M. 2009b. Barriers to movement: impacts of wind farms on migrating birds. Ices Journal of Marine Science. 66: 746–753.

Morris, R. 2009. Chase for wind power turns to Oregon's public lands. The Oregonian. May 23. http://www.oregonlive.com/environment/index.ssf/2009/05/chase_for_wind_power_turns_to.html. (30 March 2011).

National Research Council. 2007. Environmental impacts of wind-energy projects. Washington, DC: The National Academies Press. 394 p.

National Wind Coordinating Collaborative. 2010. Wind turbine interactions with birds, bats, and their habitats: a summary of research results and priority questions. Factsheet. Washington, DC. https://www.nationalwind.org/assets/publications/Birds_and_Bats_Fact_Sheet_.pdf. (30 March 2011).

Nations, C.S.; Erickson, W.P. 2009. Marbled murrelet-wind turbine collision model for the Radar Ridge wind resource area. Cheyenne, WY: Western EcoSystems Technology, Inc. 38 p.

Naugle, D.E.; Doherty, K.E.; Walker, B.L.; Holloran, M.J.; Copeland, H.E. 2011. Energy development and greater sage grouse. In: Knick, S.T.; Connelly, J.W. Greater sage-grouse: ecology and conservation of a landscape species and its habitats. Studies in Avian Biology Series (vol. 38). Berkeley, CA: University of California Press: 489–504.

Naylor, L.M.; J. Wisdom, M.; Anthony, R.G. 2009. Behavioral responses of North American elk to recreational activity. Journal of Wildlife Management. 73: 328–338.

Nelson, K.; Raphael, M.G.; Harrison, P. 2009. Independent science panel review of potential impacts to marbled murrelets relating to the Radar Ridge Wind Resource. Prepared for Commissoner of Public Lands. www.dnr.wa.gov/ publications/lm_mamu_science_panel.pdf. (June 4, 2012).

Oregon Columbia Plateau Ecoregion Wind Energy Taskforce. 2008. Oregon Columbia Plateau ecoregion wind energy siting and permitting guidelines. Portland, OR: U.S. Fish and Wildlife Service, Oregon Department of Fish and Wildlife, Oregon Department of Energy. 38 p.

Osborn, R.G.; Dieter, C.D.; Higgins, K.F.; Usgaard, R.E. 1998. Bird flight characteristics near wind turbines in Minnesota. American Midland Naturalist. 139: 29–38.

Pearce-Higgins, J.W.; Stephen, L.; Douse, A.; Langston, R.H.W. 2012. Greater impacts of wind farms on bird populations during construction than subsequent operation: results of a multi-site and multi-species analysis. Journal of Applied Ecology. 49: 386–394.

Piorkowski, M.D.; O'Connell, T.J. 2010. Spatial pattern of summer bat mortality from collisions with wind turbines in mixed-grass prairie. The American Midland Naturalist. 164: 260–269.

Popa-Lisseanu, A.G.; Voigt, C.C. 2009. Bats on the move. Journal of Mammalogy. 90: 1283–1289.

Rabin, L.A.; Coss, R.G.; Owings, D.H. 2006. The effects of wind turbines on antipredator behavior in California ground squirrels (*Spermophilus beecheyi*). Biological Conservation. 131: 410–420.

Reijnen, R.; Foppen, R.; Meeuwsen, H. 1996. The effects of traffic on the density of breeding birds in Dutch agricultural grasslands. Biological Conservation. 75: 255–260.

Renewable Northwest Project. 2011. Map of renewable energy projects in Pacific Northwest. http://www.rnp.org/project_map. (30 March 2011).

Rollins, K.; Meyerholz, D.; Johnson, G.; Capparella, A.; Loew, S. 2012. A forensic investigation into the etiology of bat mortality at a wind farm: barotrauma or traumatic injury? Veterinary Pathology Online. 49: 362–371.

Sawyer, H.; Nielson, R.M.; Lindzey, F.; McDonald, L.L. 2006. Winter habitat selection of mule deer before and during development of a natural gas field. The Journal of Wildlife Management. 70: 396–403.

Smallwood, K.S.; Rugge, L.; Morrison, M.L. 2009. Influence of behavior on bird mortality in wind energy developments. Journal of Wildlife Management. 73: 1082–1098.

Smallwood, K.S.; Thelander, C. 2008. Bird mortality in the Altamont Pass Wind Resource Area, California. Journal of Wildlife Management. 73: 1062–1071.

Smallwood, K.S.; Thelander, C.G.; Morrison, M.L.; Rugge, L.M. 2007. Burrowing owl mortality in the Altamont Pass wind resource area. Journal of Wildlife Management. 71: 1513–1524.

Smith, V. 2010. Md. wind farm developer to forgo 24 turbines. Associated Press. January 27.

Stewart, G.B.; Pullin, A.S.; Coles, C.F. 2007. Poor evidence-base for assessment of windfarm impacts on birds. Environmental Conservation. 34: 1–11.

Stienen, E.W.M.; Courtens, W.; Everaert, J.; Van De Walle, M. 2008. Sex-biased mortality of common terns in wind farm collisions. The Condor. 110: 154–157.

Strickland, M.; Arnett, E.; Erickson, W.; Johnson, D.; Johnson, G.; Morrison, M.; Schaffer, J.; Warren-Hicks, W. 2011. Comprehensive guide to studying wind Energy/wildlife interactions. Prepared for the National Wind Coordinating Collaborative, Washington, DC. 281 p. http://www.nationalwind.org/publications/comprehensiveguide.aspx. (28 March 2012).

Switalski, T.A.; Bissonette, J.A.; DeLuca, T.H.; Luce, C.H.; Madej, M.A. 2004. Benefits and impacts of road removal. Frontiers in Ecology and the Environment. 2: 21–28.

Telleria, J.L. 2009. Wind power plants and the conservation of birds and bats in Spain: a geographical assessment. Biodiversity and Conservation. 18: 1781–1791.

Trombulak, S.C.; Frissell, C.A. 2000. Review of ecological effects of roads on terrestrial and aquatic communities. Conservation Biology. 14: 18–30.

U.S. Department of Agriculture, Forest Service [USDA Forest Service]. 2011a. Special uses handbook: wind energy uses. FSH 2709.11. Chapter 70. Washington, DC.

U.S. Department of Agriculture, Forest Service [USDA Forest Service]. 2011b. Wildlife and fisheries program management handbook: wildlife monitoring at wind energy sites. FSH 2609.13. Chapter 80. Washington, DC.

U.S. Department of Energy. 2008. 20% wind energy by 2030: increasing wind energy's contribution to U.S. electricity supply. Washington, DC. 228 p.

U.S. Department of Energy. 2010. Wind power today 2010. Wind and Water Power Program. www.nrel.gov/wind/pdfs/47531.pdf. (30 March 2011).

U.S. Department of Energy. 2011. 2010 wind technologies market report. Berkeley, CA: Lawrence Berkeley National Laboratory. 84 p.

U.S. Department of Energy; U.S. Department of the Interior [USDOE and USDI]. 2008. Programmatic environmental impact statement, designation of energy corridors on federal land in the 11 western states (DOE/EIS-0386). Bureau of Land Management. http://corridoreis.anl.gov/index.cfm. (30 March 2011).

U.S. Department of the Interior, Bureau of Land Management [USDI BLM]. 2005a. Final programmatic environmental impact statement on wind energy development on BLM-administered land on the Western United States. Washington, DC. http://windeis.anl.gov. (30 March 2011).

U.S. Department of the Interior, Bureau of Land Management [USDI BLM]. 2005b. Record of Decision, Implementation of a Wind Energy Development Program and Associated Land Use Plan Amendments. Washington, DC. 42 p. http://windeis.anl.gov/documents/docs/WindPEISROD.pdf. (30 March 2011).

U.S. Department of the Interior, Bureau of Land Management [USDI BLM]. 2009. Renewable Energy and the BLM: Wind (Section 211 of Energy Policy Act). Factsheet. http://www.blm.gov/pgdata/etc/medialib/blm/wo/MINERALS__ REALTY__AND_RESOURCE_PROTECTION_/energy.Par.58306.File. dat/09factsheetmap_Wind.pdf. (30 March 2011).

U.S. Fish and Wildlife Service. 2011a. Draft Eagle Conservation Plan Guidance. http://www.fws.gov/windenergy/. (22 June 2011).

U.S. Fish and Wildlife Service. 2011b. Risk assessment tools for tier 2 and tier 3. http://www.fws.gov/windenergy/docs/Risk_Assess_Tools.pdf. (02 April 2011).

U.S. Fish and Wildlife Service. 2012. U.S. Fish and Wildlife Service land-based wind energy guidelines. http://www.fws.gov/windenergy. (28 March 2012).

Walker, B.L.; Naugle, D.E.; Doherty, K.E. 2007. Greater sage-grouse population response to energy development and habitat loss. Journal of Wildlife Management. 71: 2644–2654.

Walter, W.D.; Leslie Jr, D.M.; Jenks, J.A. 2006. Response of Rocky Mountain elk (*Cervus elaphus*) to wind-power development. The American Midland Naturalist. 156: 363–375.

Washington Department of Fish and Wildlife. 2009. Washington Department of Fish and Wildlife Wind Power Guidelines. http://wdfw.wa.gov/publications/pub. php?id=00294. (30 March 2011).

Weller, T.J.; Baldwin, J.A. 2011. Using echolocation monitoring to model bat occupancy and inform mitigations at wind energy facilities. The Journal of Wildlife Management. 76: 619–631.

Weller, T.J.; Cryan, P.M.; O'Shea, T.J. 2009. Broadening the focus of bat conservation and research in the USA for the 21st century. Endangered Species Research. 8: 129–145.

Wisdom, M.J.; Holthausen, R.S.; Wales, B.C.; Hargis, C.D.; Saab, V.A.; Lee, D.C.; Hann, W.J.; Rich, T.D.; Rowland, M.M.; Murphy, W.J.; Eames, M.R. 2000. Source habitats for terrestrial vertebrates of focus in the interior Columbia basin: broad-scale trends and management implications. Volume 1—Overview. Interior Columbia Basin Ecosystem Management Project: scientific assessment. Gen. Tech. Rep. PNW-GTR-485. Portland, OR: U.S. Department of Agriculture, Forest Service, Pacific Northwest Research Station. 156 p.

Young, D.; Poulton, V. 2009. Update on vegetation and wildlife impacts from the New Desert Claim project area. Report prepared for Desert Claim Wind Power, LLC. Cheyenne, WY: Western Ecosystems Technology, Inc. 26 p. http://www. efsec.wa.gov/Desert%20Claim/Revised%20Application/Tab%205.pdf. (30 March 2011).